N
W   E
S

Congo

ATLANTIC   OCEAN

● Loanda

SOUTH

Orang

Cape Town ●

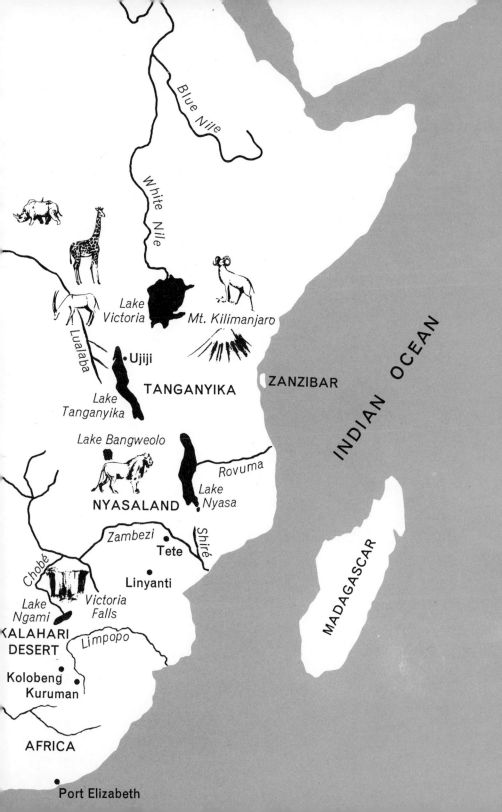

the true story of

DAVID LIVINGSTONE

the true story of

DAVID
LIVINGSTONE

EXPLORER

BY RICHARD ARNOLD

CHILDRENS PRESS, CHICAGO

American edition published through the courtesy of
Frederick Muller Limited
London

Library of Congress Catalog Card Number: 64-12909
Copyright © in Great Britain, 1957, Richard Arnold
© 1964, Childrens Press
Lithographed in the U.S.A.

Contents

Author and Artist

Richard Arnold was born in Scotland and now lives in London with his wife and son. He served with the British Army Commandos in World War II, and since then he has been a deep-sea fisherman, a circus artist, and a professional skater. He is keen on shooting, fencing, gliding, skating, and sailing. Now, as a professional sports writer, most of his books are on hunting, fishing, gun care, or camping.

Parviz Sadighian was born in Tehran, Iran, in 1939. He was graduated from the Academy of Fine Arts in Tehran and received a partial scholarship for foreign study. In 1959 he enrolled at the Art Institute in Chicago and continued his studies in sculpture and in painting. Interest in painting led to courses in illustration and advertising art. Mr. Sadighian is now associated with the Bert Ray Studio in Chicago.

Foreword

The story of David Livingstone's life is a thrilling one of adventure and cool courage.

He was the first white man to penetrate the mysterious interior of Africa. His life from 1840 to 1873 was a triumph of will power over adversity.

Slave traders, hostile natives, forest fires, foaming rapids, barren deserts, charging lions, ill-health, mutinous bearers—all added to the difficulties of mapping unknown lands and collecting information about African animals and plants.

Livingstone captured the imagination of the world and became a legend in his own lifetime. Even now the paths that Livingstone took through Africa are held in greater respect by the native peoples for the white man than other routes. More than any other man, he was instrumental in freeing Africa from the slave trade.

the true story of

DAVID LIVINGSTONE

African Magic

The countryside was parched and brown, broken only here and there by large outcrops of grey stone and a far-off range of pale blue mountains that shivered and danced in the heat-torn air. The grasses, tall as a man, stood yellow and dry; the ground, baked hard, spread endlessly with huge cracks. The sun poured down its heat from a sky devoid of clouds and brilliant in the intensity of its blue.

Across this scene, dwarfed by their surroundings, a little procession of wagons, drawn by oxen, lumbered towards the sanctuary of the distant hills; for this was Africa in the middle of the last century, when no railroads nor any other form of road existed—when Africa was, indeed, an unknown, unexplored, and unexploited region known as the Dark Continent. To travel across country was a great and daring undertaking, for not only were there natural perils to be faced but also attacks from wild animals and from even more savage natives.

In the leading wagon a white man lay sleeping uneasily in the shade of the canvas hood, oblivious to the jarring and bumping, as the huge unsprung wheels rattled and jolted over the virgin savannah. The jingle of the harness, the clump of the oxen's hoofs, and the labored creaking of the wheels were sounds that somehow seemed only to emphasize the immense silence of that vast and brooding countryside.

Abruptly the man was wakened by the sudden stopping of the wagon and a babble of excited shouts. He roused himself and pushed open the curtains at the rear of the vehicle.

"What is it?" he shouted.

But his question went unheeded, for the members of the caravan were running about in panic, shouting, gesticulating, and pointing towards the distant hills. Their dark faces, beaded with sweat, had assumed a grey pallor. The white man knew immediately that whatever had scared his followers, the panic at all costs must be stopped.

"Silence!" he roared, jumping down from the wagon and hurrying towards the jabbering natives. "What's the matter?"

18

He grabbed a tall native by the shoulder and jerked him round. "Speak!"

"*Bwana*," the man spluttered. "Fire! No escape. Look!"

The white man gazed in the direction of the outstretched hand, and for a moment an agony of fear swept through him.

Ahead of them, directly across the route his little caravan was taking, stretched a wall of fire. It was some four or five miles away but covered a front of at least two miles on either side of them.

He made a rapid calculation. He guessed the speed of the wind as he looked at the advancing wall of flame, a dull red glow from which, even at that range, sudden flames showed up, and the dense pall of smoke above it. "About twelve minutes," he thought, "at most a quarter of an hour, and then it'll be upon us. There's no time to lose!"

It was obvious to him that he could not attempt to turn and flee before the flames. Nor could he hope to drive through them; the slowness of the wagons, the speed of the oncoming fire could only result in one end. He had no wish to leave charred bones on a fire-blackened countryside as mute evidence of his passing.

"Djambi!" he shouted to one of the natives. "Ho, there, Djambi; bring me fire!"

Djambi, a tall, well-proportioned native, gaped at the white man, disbelief in his voice. "Fire, *bwana?*"

For answer the white man turned to the caravan. "Set fire to the grasses behind us. Let the wind take the fire from us. Hurry! Hurry!"

"Ah, *bwana.*" Djambi turned to the others, the plan understood, and immediately with blazing torches they set fire to the grasses and shrubs behind them. To the fierce heat of the sun was now added the scorching fury of the fire in their rear. But the wind which was bearing the dreaded savannah fire down upon them had become an ally, and presently a charred, smoking, blackened, bare patch of earth stretched for a hundred yards behind and on either side of the sweating, smoke-begrimed party.

"Make ready the wagons!" shouted the white man. "Drive them on to the burned ground; the fire will then divide and cannot touch us." But the ground was still hot, and the oxen could not be persuaded to tread it. Precious minutes passed waiting for the ground to cool. The roar and crackle of the advancing flames, now scarcely a mile away, could plainly be heard.

Standing on a heap of stones the white man could see herds of buck darting past, followed by great swarms of insects and birds, trying to escape the holocaust. To one side a pride of lions galloped in panic, while the frightened oxen tethered to the wagons pulled and tugged in vain effort to escape.

"Move the wagons!"

The terrified beasts, with great difficulty, were driven on to the burned stubble. Some fifty yards the party moved in, then cowered together to watch the roaring, rolling wall of fire bear down on them. Sparks from burning grasses falling upon the wagons were at once beaten out. Now and again, one or other of the terrified teams would rear up, instinctively seeking escape, and were restrained only with difficulty. On and on the fire swept, and the heat became suffocating. The hard blaze of the sun, suddenly cut off by the vast crowding pall of smoke, gave place to an unnatural twilight.

For what seemed an eternity to the little group the towering front of flame bore down on them. And then abruptly, as they watched, it reached the edge of the burned stubble and there halted and was defeated. To right and left, however, it roared on, followed by a sudden, intense gale, and as equally sudden a calm.

For a moment or so, the white man looked at the scene before him. Across the golden-brown countryside there now stretched a broad black scar, devoid of all life, a waste of blowing dust and ash and cinders. Behind him the men were already moving the wagons into position, ready to resume the trek, already in their African fatalism forgetful of their narrow escape from a terrible death.

He walked back to his wagon and climbed onto the buckboard, then, in answer to the driver's inquiring gaze, nodded, The long whips cracked, the oxen strained, and the great wheels resumed their rolling. The incident of the fire was over.

This was but one small episode in the life of David Livingstone, explorer, missionary and doctor, who, alone but for native companions, ill-equipped and often hindered by ill health, became a legend during his own life as one of the greatest explorers of all time, and in the missionary field came to be regarded as a second St. Paul.

The paths which Livingstone took through Africa are, to this very day, marked with greater respect for the white man than other routes. It is admitted that the great work he performed in Africa in bringing a system of education to the natives and fighting to raise their status from virtual serfdom, has become more important every year.

Measures that he advocated a hundred years ago to try to raise the whole moral tone of African life for both native and European alike—his campaign against the color bar and his insistence on the view that the natives should be regarded as potential customers and consumers and not merely underpaid or cheated producers, as well as their being brethren in the sight of God—had they been effected, would probably have avoided the bitter racial disputes which have arisen from time to time in that great continent and in South Africa in particular.

His name is perpetuated in the town of Livingstone, the capital of Northern Rhodesia, and in the Livingstone Mountains near Lake Nyasa. A new honor was accorded his memory on July 15th, 1955 when Rhodesia and Nyasaland issued special stamps to commemorate the centenary of his discovery of the Victoria Falls. Set against a picture of the mighty Falls themselves, Dr. David Livingstone's picture thus appeared on a stamp design for the first time. But, without doubt, his greatest memorial lies in the fact that he was the one man responsible for the ultimate freeing of Africa from the slave trade, and also in his initiation of sympathy and respect for the Negro in Europe. From 1840 until his death he campaigned against that terrible result of ignorance and intolerance—the color bar.

Had it not been for his peaceful penetration of the interior, there might well have been greater conflict between African and European.

He opened up part of a new world. He was the first white man many of the natives had ever seen, and the great impression he made is still remembered. But, unfortunately, though he opened up new routes to unknown regions of the African Continent, others who followed his trail, the great commercial concerns and military expeditions, disregarded his doctrines and brought indignities upon the natives, and, in turn, incurred distrust of the white man.

Had Livingstone been content to keep to a small mission station, had he elected to live the life of a simple pastor among the converted natives, the new trails into Africa would have been made by slave traders and speculators, greedy for the riches of the newly discovered territories, and they would have been followed by the military. In that event, there is little doubt that Africa would have been ablaze from end to end in bitter, unremitting war between the white and colored races.

What sort of a man was David Livingstone?

He was a Scot of humble parentage—Highlander on his father's side, Lowlander on his mother's. He was born at Blantyre in Lanarkshire on March 19th, 1813, and he wrote with pride that his paternal great-grandfather fell at Culloden fighting for Bonnie Prince Charlie, the Young Pretender.

Young David Livingstone was sent to work in a cotton-spinning factory at the age of ten, and, incredible to modern ideas, worked there from six in the morning until eight o'clock at night with only short intervals for breakfast and dinner. In the evenings he studied at a night school from eight o'clock to ten, and when he returned home, continued with his books until midnight or even later. His mother rightly objected to this and would sometimes take his books away from him and gently, but firmly, pack him off to bed.

For nearly nine years young Livingstone continued in this manner. He was not, as has often been supposed, a self-educated man, but was assisted in his studies by a schoolmaster who was so moderate in his charges that, even in those comparatively dark days by modern standards, all who wished to be taught by him might afford it.

David Livingstone used to carry on part of his studies at the mill. He would place one of his textbooks on a portion of the spinning jenny so that he could snatch sentence after sentence from it as he passed back and forth.

The din inside a cotton mill is terrific: the roar of the machinery makes it impossible for a person to hear even his own voice, and mill operatives converse with each other after the manner of deaf people by lip reading and mouthing. It was a result of having to concentrate on his studies amid the roar of machinery that Livingstone, later in life, was able to write up his journals and deal with his correspondence from home in perfect comfort, completely undisturbed by the noisy play of native children, or a tribe's dancing and singing, accompanied by resounding drums and horns.

By the time he was nineteen, he had decided that he would become a missionary and, in order to further his ambition, set

out to obtain a medical education—one of the necessary quali-
fications. His long days of toil in the cotton-spinning mill were
now over, and he enrolled as a student at Glasgow University.

It was a very difficult period for him. He had to work hard
during the summer in order to pay his college fees and main-
tain himself at the University during the winter, and he had
to practice the utmost self-denial in order to further his plans.
Whether he would have succeeded in this enterprise alone can
only be surmised, because, on the advice of friends, he joined
the London Missionary Society and through it was able to continue his medical studies as well as his divinity course.

In November, 1840, he received his medical diploma, though
his studies had been interrupted by a severe illness as a result
of his persistent overworking. He was ordained that same
month, and three weeks later sailed for Africa.

All Livingstone's early studies had been devoted to the prospect of becoming a missionary in China. Throughout his ap-
prenticeship with the London Missionary Society, his hopes and
aspirations had centered upon travels in what was then, as now,
a closed empire. But war was brewing between China and
England, and when hostilities did break out—in the disgraceful
episode of the Opium War—the directors of the Missionary
Society decided that he should go to Africa.

At first he was not enthusiastic, but chance led to a meeting
with the distinguished African missionary, Robert Moffat, who
fired Livingstone's imagination with stories of the work that was
to be done there. It was Moffat who began to bring the magic of
Africa to Livingstone, and it was he who encouraged Living-

stone in the course he was to take—namely, not to settle down in an already established station but to penetrate to the interior where neither missionary nor explorer had then set foot.

Moffat's description of the land, where in the bright light of an ordinary morning one could see the smoke of a thousand villages, completed the spell, and Livingstone let the directors of the London Missionary Society know that he was willing to go to Africa after he had passed his medical examinations.

In this modern age, Cape Town is only a few hours away from London by jet airliner; even taking the much slower steamer, the traveling time is shorter than the voyage that the ship carrying Livingstone took. When the *George*, as she was named, slipped down the Thames at the beginning of her voyage, she began a journey lasting eighty-two days. For young David Livingstone, it was the beginning of a travel adventure which was to last sixteen years before he returned home.

In spite of the lengthy voyage, in which the vessel crossed the Atlantic to Rio de Janiero and then recrossed it again to Cape Town, David Livingstone found much to interest him. The commander of the *George*, Captain Donaldson, a fellow Scot, took a great interest in the young missionary, and taught him the rudiments of navigation and how to steer a course. So well were these lessons learned that Livingstone plotted maps of his journeys into the unknown parts of Southern Africa which remain unaltered and correct even to this day.

Such then, was David Livingstone—a man of great courage, great industry, and great humanity. Typical of the man was his attitude to missionary work. In addition to his missionary

26

activities, he carried out medical work. Over and above this, he found time to make exploratory travels; labored at building and handicraft work in an effort to improve the lot of the native peoples he encountered; and, at the end of each day's labor, found time to make a detailed record not only of the things he had done but also the things he had seen.

Many of these matters were of scientific importance to the geographer; many were of great interest to the naturalist; others were of great moment to the anthropologist.

He was, a times, stubborn and sharp-tempered, but, like St. Paul, he was subject to illnesses and internal troubles brought on by overwork and the hardships to which he was exposed during his travels.

We do not know, we can only guess, at the thoughts which surged through Livingstone's mind as the distant coastline of Africa rose over the horizon and later when the little ship dropped anchor in the shadow of Table Mountain. But this we know, from his writings and his acts—that the African magic was to possess him completely.

Today his body lies beneath a simple stone in the ancient Abbey of Westminster. Nearby, his statue faces southward across the muddy, historic Thames towards that great Continent of Africa where, at Ilala in Northern Rhodesia, his heart was buried by his simple, faithful, native companions.

Attack of the Wounded Lion

The *George* was destined for discharge at Port Elizabeth on Algoa Bay, but required refitting. This meant staying a month in Table Bay, and Livingstone, with some of the other passengers whose ultimate port of disembarkation was Port Elizabeth, spent that time ashore.

It was not wasted, however. Livingstone spent as much time as possible inquiring about local conditions, learning what he could about the progress of missions in the country, assimilating as much knowledge as possible about the native population.

And in that short time he found two schools of thought in the European population of South Africa. On the one hand, there were those who befriended the colored man and believed in his ultimate rise in the social order; on the other, there were those who intended to keep the Negro in the status of semi-slavery.

This position is much the same in South Africa today, and, strangely enough, the friends of the natives were the British settlers, while the reactionaries were of Dutch stock. Inevitably, Livingstone attacked their teachings and, as we shall see later, incurred hostility from the Boers.

But Livingstone was impatient to leave Cape Town and resume the voyage to Port Elizabeth, where, on May 19th, 1841, he disembarked and started his first long overland African journey. It is hard to realize today that less than 100 years ago Africa was an uncharted continent, the maps of which contained great blanks of unknown territory. When Livingstone set out on his first trek to the missionary station at Kuruman, some 530 miles from Port Elizabeth, he was traveling upon one of the few known tracks in what was a vast wilderness.

The source of the Niger was known then—it had been discovered some ten years or so earlier—but the path of the Congo was a mystery, the Great African Lakes had not been seen by white men, the source of the Nile had yet to be discovered.

Livingstone took great delight in this first journey. He wrote glowing descriptions of the countryside, its peoples, the novelty of the trip, and his aspirations. But the traveling was rough. Roads were almost nonexistent; the only available means of transport was the covered ox wagon; and in some portions of the journey the travelers had to go on foot. In addition, detours had to be made to visit two mission stations, and it is not surprising that the party did not complete the journey until July 31st, 1841.

The policy of missionaries in Africa under the auspices of the London Missionary Society at that time was to operate from centralized stations. Livingstone, young and inexperienced as he was, thought differently. The effect of Moffat's words weighed heavily with him, and he was determined to move out into the vast unknown countryside with the object of establishing new missionary centers.

Within a few years, he had ceased to be a purely evangelical missionary and had become an explorer, though he still strove to convert the natives.

From Kuruman, he pushed 200 miles further to Mabotsa, and then progressed to Chonuane and Kolobeng, driving into the wilderness, and leaving far behind him the frontiers of advanced mission and trading posts.

Within eight weeks of arriving at Kuruman, he began to make experimental trips into lands lying to the northeast, and ultimately reached Lepelole, about 250 miles distant, in the territory of the Bakwains. It was here that he decided that a new mission station would be ideally situated.

But it was, of course, essential to obtain approval from the headquarters of the Missionary Society. Accordingly, he returned to Kuruman to make his report and recommendations. His restless spirit, however, would not allow him to await the decision of higher authority, and he decided to make another journey upcountry to Lepelole.

This time, in order to obtain an accurate knowledge of the native language and customs, he cut himself off from all European society by journeying there with but a few native servants and living among the tribesmen. During this period, he began to prepare the foundations for a settlement, to erect buildings, and to cut a canal for irrigation of the gardens.

The chief of the tribe—the Bakwains, a branch of the Bechuanas—was an amiable native called Bubi. He made Livingstone very welcome, and Livingstone made special note of the fact that during the six months or so that he was living among the Bakwains nothing was ever stolen from him—he found them a scrupulously honest people. Ironically enough, he found later that in regions where the African had come into contact with the Arab slaver, or even with European traders, he found thieving rampant.

Leaving Bubi in charge of building the mission, Livingstone set out for the north to visit the Bakaa and the Bamangwato, and here he ran into his first trouble with the natives.

A trader and his little caravan, moving northward into the territory of the Bakaa, fell foul of the tribe, and in the resultant collision the trader and all his followers were murdered. The sudden appearance of Livingstone, fairly recently after this unfortunate tragedy, convinced the Bakaa that they were to be punished, and, accordingly they prepared to resist.

When Livingstone rode into the village, one false move would have meant his death. Hundreds of suspicious tribesmen, lurking in hiding places, grasping spear and ax, awaited the signal to fall upon the intruder and hack him to death. If Livingstone was aware of the danger he gave no sign of it. He walked steadily on into the center of the village, saluted the chief, and partook of the food supplied to him.

One sign of fear, one act of arrogance, would have been the end, but Livingstone behaved with supreme coolness and forbearance. He ordered his followers to set up camp *in the village itself,* and then, observed by hostile warriors ready to strike, calmly lay down to rest!

After a little while, though it must have seemed an age to the white man, the natives came from their hiding places, and somewhat shamefacedly offered signs of friendship. The danger was over, and within a few moments Livingstone was preaching to them in the Sichuana language, which he had so earnestly studied in his voluntary exile a few months before.

He remained with the Bakaa for a short time and then continued his trek to the Bamangwato and Makalaka tribes. With the Bamangwato he met Sekhomi, the father of Khama, who was one of the most famous of all African chiefs and a direct ancestor of Seretse Khama, who, only a few years ago, was exiled from his tribe because he had married a white woman. Sekhomi gave Livingstone an enthusiastic welcome, and provided him with porters for his journey. It was on this trip that the missionary penetrated to within ten miles of Lake Ngami, which he was later to discover.

Much of the journey, however, had to be undertaken on foot because many of the draft oxen were sick, and he turned back to Kuruman to complete a journey of more than a thousand miles in less than six months.

No sooner had Livingstone arrived back at Kuruman than tribal warfare blazed up, and the Bakwains were driven from Lepelole by marauding tribes. The whole countryside was filled with war parties, and it was unsafe for any European to attempt to travel through those regions without a retinue of guides, carriers, and soldiers. In the meantime, therefore, Livingstone went ahead with his plans to found a missionary station in the beautiful valley of Mabotsa, to which region he moved when the countryside became peaceful.

Mabotsa was the scene of perhaps one of the most famous of all Livingstone incidents, for it was here that he was attacked and mauled by a wounded lion. The people of the Bakatla tribe, who lived in the village of Mabotsa, were troubled by the lions that leaped the stockades of their cattle pens and destroyed their cows and sheep. Even more unusual, the lions attacked the herds in open daylight, and, as a result, the Bakatla, who were a rather cowardly people, believed that they had been bewitched and given into the power of a neighboring tribe.

When Livingstone was told about this he showed great indignation. "Bewitched!" he roared. "Nonsense! The next time your herds are attacked, I'll come with you. I'll help you rid yourselves of these beasts."

34

The next day, the lions attacked again and destroyed nine sheep. "Come," said Livingstone to the native hunters, "we will seek out the lions and destroy them, or drive them away from this district."

Encouraged by the white man, the hunters soon tracked down the lions to a small wood on a hillock, and, forming a circle round the beasts—a traditional African way of hunting—gradually closed in to spear them. Unfortunately, the Bakatla lost their nerve, and when one of the lions charged, the hunters broke ranks and allowed it to escape, to be followed a few seconds after by the flashing, tawny bodies of its companions.

Livingstone, who was standing a little way down the hillside with a native schoolmaster named Mebalwe, wanted to take a shot at the escaping beasts, but he could not fire for fear of hitting the hunters. He lowered his gun and sighed as he turned to his native companion. "Come on, Mebalwe," he said, "let's go back to the village; they're a poor lot these Bakatla . . ."

Scarcely had the pair of them turned and started to descend the hill when the harsh coughing roar of a lion sounded near at hand. They stopped at once, bringing their guns into the ready position. "Steady, *bwana*," cautioned Mebalwe, pointing to a thick thorn bush, "*Simba*, he behind there; he wounded, no good."

About fifteen yards ahead of them Livingstone could see the tawny shape of a lion, partly concealed by the bush. He could see the black-tipped tail lashing in fury. Slowly he raised his gun and aimed it where he presumed the heart of the beast to be, then squeezed first the right and then the left trigger. For a brief moment lion and bush were hidden from the doctor by the cloud of smoke from the gun, and at the same time he heard the tribesmen rushing down the hillside screaming, "Hurrah, it is dead! It is dead!"

Livingstone stepped back a little and began to reload his gun. "Don't rush in!" he shouted to the natives, "He may not be dead. . . !" Then he turned again to the act of pouring the powder down the muzzle. A sudden shout caused him to lift his head, and, in that moment, he saw the lion springing upon him. Down they went to the ground together, man and beast. Growling fiercely, the lion bit into Livingstone's shoulder and began to shake him as a terrier shakes a rat.

Mebalwe ran to within a few feet of the beast and pulled the triggers of his gun, but it misfired, and the lion, leaving Livingstone, turned on his new foe and bit him in the thigh. A second native, whose life Livingstone had saved some time earlier after he had been tossed by a buffalo, ran in with his spear, but he, too, was attacked by the lion. A third native went to the assistance of the three wounded men, and at that moment the bullets took effect and the lion dropped dead.

Gently, tenderly, the Bakatla bore their comrades and their white leader back to the village, after which they returned for the carcass of the lion. Livingstone records that it was the largest ever killed in the district, and that the Bakatla, to break the alleged "spell" put upon them and to drive the witchcraft from the lion, burned it in a large bonfire.

For a long time, Livingstone's life hung in the balance, and he suffered terribly. The lion left him with eleven ugly gashes and a shattered arm, but the nursing of the natives and the attention he received from a fellow missionary, Edwards, saved his life, though the upper part of his arm was so injured that for the remainder of his life he could never raise a gun to the level of his shoulder without steadying the barrel against some support.

The two natives, who were even more badly injured, both survived their ordeal, and the steadfast and loyal Mebalwe continued in Livingstone's service for a long time.

When he had sufficiently recovered, Livingstone returned to Kuruman for convalescent treatment. As soon as he was fit enough to ride on horseback again, he journeyed over 150 miles to the south to welcome Robert Moffat and his family, who had just returned from a long leave in England.

Fate seemed to have bound up the name of Moffat inextricably with that of Livingstone. In the first place, Moffat had encouraged him to travel to Africa and take up work there. But there was a second result. The journey Livingstone undertook to meet the Moffats ended by his falling in love with Mr. Moffat's daughter Mary, whom he later married.

From the time of their marriage until her death seventeen years later, Mary and her husband worked together with a devotion that has seldom been surpassed. Together they shared the toils and privations of journeys into strange lands; they experienced drought, famine, hostility from natives and Dutch settlers; and together they opened up new lands, discovered new peoples. The story of David Livingstone is also the story of Mary, his wife.

Conqueror of the Desert

After his marriage in January, 1845, Livingstone took his wife to Mabotsa. There he intended to make the new mission station into a center similar to Kuruman. But this ambition was to be denied him.

His missionary companion, Edwards, who had nursed him after the attack from the lion, was a man some eighteen years older than Livingstone. Furthermore, he had his own set ideas on how to deal with the natives and how to further the aims of the Missionary Society.

Livingstone could never be accused of being either tactful or easy going. He, too, had his own ideas on how a missionary station should be run, and, in consequence, there was a serious clash of personalities.

Edwards thought that Livingstone took too much upon himself without consulting superiors, and a certain amount of jealousy of the younger man appears in a complaint Edwards made to the directors of the London Missionary Society in which he stated that he did not wish to be treated as "an appendix" of Livingstone.

Relations gradually became worse between the two fellow workers, and Livingstone and his wife finally decided that the wisest course would be to move from Mabotsa and set up another station elsewhere. As he was already working among the Bakwains, Livingstone thought he would move to Chonuane, some forty miles away, where he could continue his work undisturbed and in his own fashion.

Sechele, chief of the tribe, and Livingstone had already known each other some years. A great bond of affection existed between the native prince and the missionary, based primarily on the fact that the latter had cured Sechele's child of a disease. Sechele was a most loyal friend and a firm convert to Christianity, though in the long periods of drought which his tribe suffered from time to time he was apt to ask Livingstone for permission to make rain-doctor magic—a request which Livingstone, naturally enough, always refused.

Also typical of Sechele was the fact that he learned the alphabet in one day and then suggested to Livingstone that it was a waste of time preaching to his tribe and spending so much time trying to convert them.

"Do you really think that my people will ever believe what you say by just talking to them?" he once asked the missionary. "I can only make them do anything by beating them. Let me summon my head man, and with our *litupa* (rhinoceros-hide whips) we'll make them all believe in no time."

The Livingstones moved to Chonuane early in 1846, but during the first season there was a terrible drought, in addition to which the area was subject to raids by marauding tribes and the hostility of the neighboring Dutch settlers.

In February the following year, Livingstone managed to convince Sechele that the tribe should move to the River Kolobeng, about forty miles away, where water could be obtained to irrigate the lands. Under Livingstone's direction the Bakwains dammed the river, made a canal and also built a school. But even in this new location, bad luck dogged Livingstone's footsteps. For the following year no rain fell, though rain could often be seen falling on a range of hills only ten miles away.

In the third year, the same extraordinary drought continued and the Kolobeng ran dry. To make matters worse, the rainmakers and witchdoctors began to complain that the hardships they suffered were due to Livingstone.

With the drought came famine. The tribesmen scoured the countryside for wild fruits and plants; their hunting parties went far afield after wild game. The mission became dependent on Kuruman for supplies of corn, and at one period Livingstone and his family—there were now three children—were reduced to living on bran, locusts, caterpillars and a species of very large frog known as "Matlametlo." The latter, when cooked, looked and tasted like chicken.

At this time, also, the Boers were building up a propaganda campaign against Livingstone and the Bakwains. Livingstone they accused of gunrunning, of inciting the natives to slay the Boers, and of being in possession of a cannon. In actual fact, the Bakwains possessed but five muskets, which Sechele had purchased from English traders, and the so-called "cannon" was nothing more or less than an iron cooking pot which Livingstone had loaned to the chief.

The Boers were Dutch colonists of South Africa, engaged in agriculture and livestock raising. Their first settlement at the Cape of Good Hope dated from the sixteenth century, but their numbers had been reinforced by Huguenots from France.

In 1814, the Cape of Good Hope became British. British policy was, of course, based on the fundamental rule of English law that there is no distinction between colored men and white. Furthermore, the Hottentot slaves of the Boers were emancipated, and this was, so far as the Boers were concerned, the last straw.

They felt aggrieved by their loss of "property" in their slaves, and in 1835, they began the Great Trek northward to Natal, the Orange Free State and the Transvaal. Here they established Republics, where they carried on their policy of "proper treatment of the Negroes," which was, in essence, compulsory, unpaid labor.

Sechele and his tribe had witnessed the spectacle of various neighboring tribes brought into slavery by the neighboring Boers. The Bakatla, the Batlokua, the Bahukeng, the Bamosetla and two other lesser tribes were groaning under Boer oppression. Livingstone, himself, records:

"I have myself been an eyewitness of Boers coming to a village, and, according to their usual custom, demanding twenty or thirty women to weed their gardens, and have seen these women proceed to the scene of unrequited toil, carrying their own food on their heads, their children on their backs, and instruments of labor on their shoulders."

When Livingstone remonstrated with Commandant Kruger about these practices and also sought permission to establish missionary centers in Boer territory, he was told that no attempt at evangelization was to be permitted among the natives. And, furthermore, *any native teacher operating in or near to their territory would be killed.*

Livingstone, through his friendship with Sechele and the support he gave the chief, was thus a thorn in the sides of the Boers, who sought every means they could to discredit him and have him removed.

The charge that Livingstone was supplying guns to the natives was ridiculous, but Livingstone was very careful to point out that, though the Boers enacted stern legislation against the trading of arms and ammunition to the natives, he often came across Boer traders in Kolobeng trying to sell muskets and powder to the tribesmen. Whether it was open trading or an attempt to place arms in the hands of the natives and then accuse Livingstone of supplying them, we do not know.

Livingstone protested, in vain, to the British administrators at the Cape against the Boer persecution. The authorities were loath to intervene on the side of the natives against the Dutch settlers and were unwilling to offend the Boers.

Encouraged by this official apathy, the demands of the Boers increased—and Sechele found himself compelled to hand over hostages—in reality, slaves—to the Boers as guarantees of his own good behavior. One of the chief's own children was carried off by a marauding party of Dutch settlers, and though Livingstone tried hard, he was unable to have the child restored, nor could he obtain any compensation for the wrongs inflicted.

Ironically enough, at the present day the teachings and ideas of these stubborn, extremely bigoted settlers have prevailed. Livingstone's work has become a mockery in the Cape, in the Union of South Africa, where the policy of the Government there is to subjugate the colored and native peoples, to deny them the fundamental rights of citizenship, to treat them as animals and to impose the terrible policy of *apartheid*, or racial segregation.

The early Dutch settlers, full of religious spirit, regarded themselves as the chosen people of God, somewhat in the same manner of the old Israelites. They regarded the natives in the same light that the heathens were regarded by the Jews, and they saw themselves as the rod of divine vengeance.

But, as Livingstone discovered, their bigoted doctrine became tempered with commercial ideals, and in this "divine vengeance" the later Boers saw wonderful opportunities to obtain free labor, and excellent chances of enriching themselves at the expense of the native peoples, whom they officially described as "property" or "creatures."

Such, then, were the people menacing Sechele's tribe and Livingstone himself. Perhaps it is hard for us to realize just how great that menace was, but as an instance it should be quoted that whenever any form of trouble showed in a tribe, the Boers took it as an excuse to indulge in bloody massacres.

In Bechuanaland, the Boers found considerable native opposition to their methods. Lesser tribes were apt to give in meekly, allow their fellows to be taken into slavery. Not so the Bechuanas. Never, in the history of the Bechuana people, had a ruler sold any of his tribe into slavery.

In order to seize slaves for unpaid labor, the Boers resorted to the age-old political trick of spreading tales of intended uprising, then dispatching a commando to the scene of the alleged trouble, taking as many native children as possible for "hostages," or slaves, carrying off cattle and other booty and shooting down in cold blood all who sought to oppose them, irrespective of sex, or inferior armaments.

As Livingstone so rightly pointed out when he complained to the British authorities, there was no record of any Bechuanas ever engaging in offensive war with Europeans.

In 1848, the Boer Commandant and David Livingstone came face to face. A commando was being raised to subjugate the

Bakwains, and Livingstone hurried to the Boer headquarters, three hundred miles away to prevent the operation.

A large force of several hundred Boers had already been raised, and the commando was on the point of riding. However, Livingstone managed to persuade Kruger to call it off. The Boers tried hard to get Livingstone to agree to act as their *spy*. Naturally, Livingstone refused this suggestion contemptuously, and from that moment he became a marked man.

The Boers were not to be done out of their operation, however, and several more raids took place against Sechele's neighbors. The Boer plan was simple, though cruel. They forced unarmed tribes to accompany them on their raids, and, on reaching the village to be attacked, ranged the natives in front of them as a shield. Behind this human cover, they would then open fire until the villagers either fled and left their cattle, wives and children to the captors or were all wiped out.

News of these raids spread rapidly among the Bakwains, and in the wake of each the Boers sent messages to Sechele calling upon him to surrender himself to them, and above all to stop English traders from proceeding into his country.

Each time, however, Sechele, with gestures, told the Boers, "The English are my friends. I was placed here by God and not by you. I have never been conquered, nor will I ever yield to you."

All this led to a momentous decision by Livingstone. He was determined to find a more secure location for his station than the threatened Kolobeng. The road to the east was blocked by Kruger and his Boers; to the north was the great and dreaded

46

Kalahari Desert; but beyond that desert dwelt a strong chief, Sebituane, ruler of the Makololo, who might afford them protection and friendship.

Sebituane was well known to Sechele, for, when the latter was but a boy, his father had been murdered by an underchief and the boy himself held prisoner. Sebituane had come to his aid, attacked the town, killed the usurper and rescued the boy, who was then installed as chief. The ties between the two were very strong.

Livingstone, therefore, asked Sechele if he would be willing to accompany him on a trek to the north into Sebituane's territory, where they would be safe from the impending attack of the Boers. Sechele readily agreed, and plans were made for the evacuation of Kolobeng.

Little did he realize it at the time, but from that moment when he made his decision, Livingstone was to begin his work as an explorer. His phase as a settled missionary was ending.

The expedition started out on June 1st, 1849. Sechele, however, fearing the much-talked-of assault by the Boers decided that it was his duty to remain with his people. Fortunately, however, Livingstone had broached the idea of the journey to an African traveler, Colonel Steele who, in turn, had passed on the information to two big game hunters, Major Vardon and Mr. Cotton Oswell.

The two hunters were desirous of crossing the Kalahari in order to hunt elephants, and the idea of exploring new territory appealed to them. When they asked Livingstone for permission to accompany him, he very gladly acceded to their request.

Sechele furnished guides, and Mr. Oswell, who brought a companion, Murray, with him defrayed the entire expenses of the guides as well as a considerable portion of the supplies.

The Kalahari was the great barrier which had hitherto prevented access to the well-watered and fertile regions beyond. But though desert by name because it contains no *running* water and very little water in wells, this vast region is by no means destitute of vegetation. It is covered with grasses and a great variety of creeping plants, in addition to which there are areas covered by bushes and trees. It is an elevated basin between 3,000 and 4,000 feet in height and is remarkably flat, though intersected in different parts by dried-up beds of ancient rivers. Herds of antelopes roam over its plains, and form the chief quarry of its inhabitants, the Bushmen and the Bakalahari.

There is a variable rainfall over this region, and in some seasons, in addition to the vast quantities of grasses which grow there, great areas of the countryside are covered by watermelons on which the wild game feed. Ostriches, ocelots, various species of buck, and jackals abound, particularly in the northern areas.

The secret wells of the desert were known only to the Bushmen and Bakahalari; strangers were not encouraged, and often the poisoned arrows of the primitive tribesmen were sufficient discouragement, without taking into account the natural perils which had to be overcome.

Such was the desert which Livingstone and his companions were about to attempt to cross and which, for two months, thirsty, weary and exhausted, they fought.

On one occasion Oswell and Murray, accompanied by a native Bakahalari, set out to hunt some eland. The country they were in was perfectly flat and composed of soft white sand. In the bright glare of the sun, the whole countryside lost all identity marks, and it was possible to get lost only a quarter of a mile from the camp. This, indeed, happened to the hunting party, and it was not until the following day that they managed to find their way back.

They had heard stories of a vast stretch of water, an inland sea, which lay ahead of them, unbeheld by any white man. Day after day they were deceived by mirages rippling on the horizon, in which vast expanses of water, with waves dancing in the sunlight and cool, green trees reflected in the surface, caused even the horses and hunting dogs, as well as the natives themselves, to run in their direction.

On one occasion, Oswell saddled his horse to pursue a herd of elephants, but a break in the haze revealed it to have been but a mirage.

At length, on July 4th, the party reached a river, the Zouga, on the other bank of which was a small native village. In great excitement the party crossed over, though Oswell's horse bogged down, and was extracted only with great difficulty. They found the natives friendly and hospitable.

In response to the explorers' questions, the natives told them that the water flowed from the Ngami. This was indeed great news. No longer was there any need to struggle across a trackless desert. By ascending the river, they would at last reach the great lake.

However, Sekhomi of the Bamangwato, who had tried, in vain, to prevent the expedition setting out from Kolobeng, sent messengers ahead to warn the inhabitants of this region that Livingstone and his friends were out for plunder, were not to be trusted, wanted slaves. The natural prejudice which this created had to be countered, though Livingstone gradually overcame it by patience and fair dealing.

They traveled about ninety-six miles up the river and reached the town of Ngabisane, whose chief gave them every possible assistance. They were provided with primitive canoes hollowed out from tree trunks, and after twelve days of traveling in this manner, on August 1st, 1849, the travelers came to the northeast end of Lake Ngami. It was a wonderful moment for all of them, Livingstone in particular. They were gazing upon something which no other white man had ever seen—a vast sheet of water lost into limitless bounds.

But a further check occurred here. At the point where the Zouga issued from Lake Ngami, a small tribe, under the leadership of a young chief named Lechulatebe, most effectively blocked their further journey towards Sebituane.

Two hundred miles of wild country lay between Lechulatebe's village and Sebituane's tribe. He refused to supply guides. He stationed armed pickets to prevent Livingstone and his companions from crossing over to the opposite bank, and made it impossible for Livingstone to proceed.

There was nothing to do but abandon the effort for the time being and return to Kolobeng in order to re-equip another expedition and return later. On October 10th, 1849, after a further arduous journey across the Kalahari, the party reached Kolobeng.

Oswell and Murray left Livingstone and went on to Cape Town in order to get together the necessary equipment and supplies for a further attempt to reach Sebituane. Livingstone, in the meantime, reported his discovery to the London Missionary Society and to his friend Colonel Steele. Colonel Steele, in turn, reported the matter to the Royal Geographical Society, and that body gave Livingstone his first official recognition in the form of a gift of twenty-five guineas (about $127.00) and public thanks.

If this sum does not seem large in present-day eyes, it is as well to contrast the attitude of the London Missionary Society when Livingstone approached them for a building grant after he established his station at Chonuane. He asked for thirty pounds (about $150.00) and this was refused!

As this resulted in the severe privations endured by his wife, family, and himself at the time, there is little wonder that he was gradually lost to the Missionary Society.

Livingstone was impetuous. He did not wait for Oswell and Murray to return from Cape Town. In April, 1850, he set out to transplant his wife, family, and native associates to Sebituane's territory. Accompanied by Sechele, David and Mrs. Livingstone and their three children set out to cross the Kalahari and the Zouga River. Dr. and Mrs. Moffat strenuously opposed Livingstone's plan, and sought to prevail upon him to remain with the Bakwains. As it was, he was to expose his wife and children to a lot of unnecessary suffering.

The hardships of the journey itself were severe enough for the young wife and children, but worse was in store. When they reached Lechulatebe's village they found that a party of English ivory hunters were camped in the area, all stricken with malaria. They journeyed down to give what assistance they could, only to learn that one of the party had died. Livingstone's two younger children were attacked by the fever, and the following day all his servants were laid low by the same complaint. There was nothing to do, under the circumstances, but to abandon the expedition and return to Kolobeng.

Sechele had used his influence and Livingstone his hard bargaining powers to obtain Lechulatebe's permission to cross the Zouga and provide guides to reach Sebituane. To this end, he had parted with a much-prized gun to the chief, an unnecessary sacrifice as events proved.

Mrs. Livingstone had not, up to that time, even seen Lake Ngami—some six miles away—she was so busy nursing the sick, and it was only as the party was leaving that Livingstone took her on a special trip to see it.

In addition to their troubles, their cattle were attacked by the tsetse fly, and the starting back could not be delayed. However, once the invalids reached the pure air of the desert, they soon recovered. During this desert journey, they encountered Oswell travling north with a well-furnished hunting safari, and he characteristically and generously turned back at once and escorted Livingstone and his party to Kolobeng.

Shortly after she returned home to Kolobeng, Mrs. Livingstone, dreadfully exhausted as a result of the hardships she had endured, gave birth to a fourth child, Elizabeth, who died after a few weeks. Poor Mary Livingstone, seriously ill, was stricken by paralysis down one side of the face, so the whole family went to the Moffats at Kuruman for a much-needed rest and care.

Livingstone, however, with native Scottish determination, was set on making a fresh start for the Makololo territory. Accordingly, on April 8th, 1851, with an expedition equipped at the expense of Oswell, he set out on his third attempt to reach Sebituane.

Dr. Moffat protested against Livingstone taking his family with him, in view of what had happened on the previous occasion. Moffat was thinking of his daughter; Livingstone was thinking of establishing his permanent home with Sebituane's tribe. Already, as Moffat pointed out to the missionary-explorer, the last trip had nearly proved fatal to all concerned; it had actually cost him the life of his latest-born child; did he want to risk it again?

At this point, the only serious criticism that has been made against Livingstone seems fully founded. In his attitude, Livingstone showed a peculiar lack of consideration for others.

This third, and finally successful, journey to the north was filled with more pains and perils than the other two put together. The party became lost in the dreaded Kalahari, owing to the error of a bushman guide, and nearly perished with thirst. The children, in particular, suffered terribly.

Fortunately, however, the advance party of native warriors returned on the fifth afternoon of their ordeal with a few drops of water obtained from some impure source, and this undoubtedly saved their lives.

The travelers were subjected to the attacks of wild beasts and snakes. The children were covered with sores from the bites and stings of ferocious insects. The cattle were decimated by the attacks of the tsetse fly. But, in July, the party finally reached the Chobé river, within the jurisdiction of Sebituane and the Makololo tribe, some five hundred miles from Kolobeng. Here they were warmly welcomed by Sebituane himself, the greatest warrior of his day and, as Livingstone wrote: "The best specimen of a native chief I ever met."

Journey's end was a severe disappointment.

Sebituane died of pneumonia within a few days of the party's arrival. Not only was this a great blow to the expedition but a positive danger as well, because it was possible for the grief-stricken Makololo to charge Livingstone and his companions with witchcraft. Happily, however, this apprehension proved to be groundless.

The chieftainship fell upon Sebituane's daughter, Ma-mo-chisane, and she readily agreed to assist Livingstone to explore further with a view to settlement, and promised to afford him whatever facilities might be necessary.

The region was unhealthy. Livingstone could find no part of the district free from fever. Worried about their health, with the shadow of little Elizabeth on his mind, persuaded by Oswell, he decided to return to Kolobeng.

Accordingly they set out from the Makololo country on August 13th, 1851, and one month later, on September 15th,

Mrs. Livingstone gave birth to a fifth child, a boy, who was christened William Oswell in honor of their staunch and generous friend.

This leaves little wonder that Mary Livingstone was not to live many more years. She had been exposed to two terrible journeys across the Kalahari Desert, lived for a period, without any of the amenities of civilization, among primitive natives, and finally in a dreadfully weakened physical condition, had gone through the ordeal of childbirth in the middle of the desert itself.

Events made Livingstone decide that the time had come to send his family home to England, and in April, 1852, they made the 600-mile journey from Kolobeng to Cape Town, where he placed them on a homeward-bound ship and promised to rejoin them in two years. As subsequent events happened, nearly five years passed before they saw each other again.

But Livingstone had not contemplated, even for a moment, the abandonment of his enterprise. He was strengthened in his resolution because he had, for the first time, been brought into close contact with the slave trade proper during his sojourn with the Makololo. He was determined to destroy this evil and to this end sought to set a stream of legitimate commerce going. He wanted to familiarize the natives with the British way of life and thought; he wanted to bring Christian civilization into Central Africa.

"I will open a way to the interior," he wrote to his brother-in-law, J. S. Moffat, *"or perish."*

A Commando Attack!

When Mrs. Livingstone and her four children sailed from Cape Town aboard the *Trafalgar* on April 23rd, 1852, David Livingstone planned to make a temporary home in Kolobeng from which he would extend his missionary activities and carry on exploratory travels. To that end he spent three months in re-equipping himself before setting back for Kuruman.

The insidious propaganda which the Boers had circulated,

charging him as a gunrunner and stirrer-up of insurrections had borne fruit. Shortsighted Government officials, fearful of doing anything which might upset the Boers and half believing their calumnies, granted Livingstone only a very small quantity of arms and ammunition—far less, in fact, than were necessary for his requirements.

It must be remembered that both missionaries and traders carried firearms, not so much for personal protection but in order to provide themselves with food. When a caravan traveled through the wild African countryside, to a great extent it had to live off the country. An incredible amount of meat was eaten by both native bearers and the white men themselves, and shooting of game for food supplies was essential.

The journey back to Kuruman was a lengthy one, filled with many delays owing to the inadequacy of transport. At Kuruman Livingstone encountered a further halt—fortunately, as it happened—when one of his wagon wheels broke, and it was a full two weeks before he was able to set out for Kolobeng.

At the end of that period, he received a letter, brought to him personally by Masebele, the wife of Sechele. We can imagine his feelings of mingled sorrow and anger when he read that tragic note.

The letter informed him that a Boer commando, consisting of 600 mounted Boers and accompanied by several hundred natives, had appeared in the Bakwain country on September 27th. A party of Boers, with four wagons, was detached from the main body and sent to plunder Livingstone's house at Kolobeng, about eight miles north of the town of Secheli. This they did with zest, destroying his books, medicines, and surgical instruments, and carrying off or burning all his personal furniture and other property. They also took away or destroyed the stores and cattle of some English travelers who were away exploring Sebituane's country.

This was a serious blow, not only to Livingstone but to the travelers, because relays of cattle were absolutely necessary for any journey to be undertaken.

While the Boers were plundering Livingstone's home, the main body of the commando concentrated on the town of Secheli. Arrogantly, they called upon Sechele to surrender to them; threateningly, they told him to prevent the English from passing through his territory. Proudly, defiantly, Sechele told them he could do neither of these things.

It was a Saturday when the Boer force encircled the town. From their wagons they brought guns and ammunition, and with them they had also brought a swivel-gun, or cannon, which they trained upon the town center. Sechele sent a messenger to them telling them not to fight on the following day, a Sunday, and to this the invaders agreed.

On the Sunday, the Boers swaggered into the town. They even attended the Church service and heard Mebalwe, the native school teacher who had been mauled with Livingstone in the incident with the lion, preach. But there was a terrible aftermath, for at dawn on the Monday morning they opened fire on the town, raking it with musket and cannon.

Within a short time, the whole town was on fire and Sechele's warriors had to retire to a position on a small conical hill in the town center. There they held out for a whole day, and when the darkness of night fell, the Boers were glad to draw off.

Masabele herself had been hidden in a cleft of a rock immediately underneath a party of Boers. She could see the muzzles of their guns above her head, and in her arms she held her baby, who began to cry. In this alarming position, fearful of what might happen if the crying of the baby attracted the attention of the Boers, she took off her bracelets and kept the terrified child quiet until the Boers withdrew.

Many native women and children were shot by the Boers during this wanton attack. Sixty Bakwains were killed, and many women, children, and men were carried off, including one of Sechele's wives. The Boers drove off all the cattle and took away the possessions of the tribesmen. What they could not carry off they destroyed by burning. They even destroyed the standing crops.

The Boers did not get away unscathed, however, and Livingstone reported that they lost thirty-five men, "probably killed by weapons which their own community had sold" to the Bakwains.

Mebalwe, being a colored teacher, was a special target of hatred for the Boers. Though they had gone to his church for worship the day before the attack, they did their best to kill him. In spite of the many guns trained on him and the hail of bullets which whistled about him, he managed to escape, though he lost all his possessions.

Sechele fortunately escaped unscathed, though two of his children had been kidnapped.

In spite of his heavy loss and the destruction of his home, Livingstone, with his typical philosophy, remarked that perhaps it wasn't a bad thing after all; there was no longer any native in the country who did not know whose side he was on!

Naturally, he protested to the Lieutenant Governor and presented him with full details of the outrage. But British Colonial policy being what it was, nothing was done. The Boers went unchecked, and the way was paved for further bloodshed.

As a direct result of this raid, Livingstone was unable to procure any bearers to accompany him to the north, and he was detained for several months at Kuruman from sheer inability to get wagon drivers. An indirect result was that Livingstone, undeterred by this misfortune, decided that he would no longer have a permanent station.

His desire to open up the interior, which the Boers were determined to keep closed, was strengthened. He felt himself freed from the shackles of convention and resolved to set out on his travels at the earliest possible moment, in spite of the threats of vengeance which the Boers threw at him.

On November 20th, with a native trader, George Fleming, and a retinue of servants—the worst possible specimens of those who inherited all the vices and none of the virtues of the Europeans with whom they had come into contact—Livingstone set out for Linyanti. On the journey they met Sechele who was on his way to see the Queen of England to make his personal protest to her about the Boer massacre.

No more loyal friend of Britain existed in Africa at that time than Sechele, and it was with great sorrow that Livingstone tried to discourage him. Sechele, however, traveled as far as Cape Town in the hope of making his way to London. On his journey he fell in with a party of English officers returning from a battle with the Basutos at Bloemfontein, and they collected a handsome sum of money to help pay his passage.

Unfortunately, by the time Sechele reached the Cape, his means had been exhausted, and he had to make the return journey of over a thousand miles with his object unaccomplished.

Livingstone continued northward along the Kalahari, and making a wide detour to avoid falling in with the Boers, finally reached Secheli on December 31st. Here he found the Bakwains, on the verge of starvation, restless with anger against the Boers.

Sechele had given orders to his people that while he was away no act of revenge was to be perpetrated, but one little incident that flared up showed the mettle of the tribesmen. A company of Bakwains went out and surrounded a party of Boers returning from a hunting trip. When the alarmed settlers found themselves face-to-face with the haggard, vengeful natives, they begged for peace!

Livingstone was present at the incident, and the terms were clear—peace only on condition that Sechele's children were restored to him. As strong parties of Bakwains occupied every pass and gorge in the hills, the Boers had to capitulate, and the Commandment, Scholz, who had taken Sechele's children to be his own domestic slaves, had to return them.

Livingstone saw the children restored to their mother, and he noted with disgust that a very young child bore signs of untreated burns received in the battle some three months earlier.

Five days later, Livingstone resumed his march northward, and after five months of traveling reached Linyanti, the capital town of the Makololo, on May 23rd, 1853.

He was given a royal welcome. The whole population turned out to greet him, not only because they were old friends but also because the presence of a white man would, they hoped, deter the ferocious Matabele from waging war on them and discourage the dreaded Arab slave traders, whose incursions were becoming more frequent.

Ma-mochisane had abdicated in favor of her brother, Seke-letu, a lad of eighteen, giving the reason that she preferred her own home and children to the management of a tribe.

Within a week, Livingstone was struck down with fever for the first time, but, with his customary doggedness, as soon as he had recovered, he started on a further trip into the interior, searching for a healthy location for a new missionary center. In spite of the fertile countryside, rich in food-producing plants and full of game, the area was unsuited for Europeans. The heavy rains, incessant flooding, and the presence of mosquitoes —which Livingstone recorded as "showing, as they always do, the presence of malaria"—caused him to abandon this enterprise.

Furthermore, he found many of the natives barbarous in the extreme, and many of their practices shocked and nauseated him. He therefore turned his eyes towards the west. The east was out of the question, owing to the barring of the way by the Boers; the north was impassable through Portuguese and Zulu territories; the Kalahari Desert (in spite of the fact that Livingstone and others after him had crossed it) was a great natural barrier to the south. He therefore planned a daring journey of 1,500 miles to St. Paul de Loanda, approximately 200 miles south of the mouth of the Congo on the west coast of Africa.

In the meantime, the trading station that he had helped Fleming establish had to be abandoned, and Fleming sent back to Kuruman. The dishonesty and incompetence of the native assistants whom Fleming had introduced were chiefly to blame for this sorry event.

While Livingstone was at Linyanti, he was, unwittingly, the means of saving Sekeletu's life. Mpepe, half brother of Sekeletu had planned to assassinate him and take over the chieftainship. To further this end, he had entered into negotiations with the Mambari—half-caste Portuguese slave traders—to support him in return for his assistance in furthering the trade. The arrival of Livingstone alarmed the Mambari, and they withdrew to the north.

Mpepe decided to carry out his plan, with the aid of his followers, in spite of this defection, and entered Sekeletu's camp at the head of armed followers. The intention of Mpepe had been to strike down Sekeletu with his war-ax during their ensuing conference, and this was to be the signal for a general insurrection.

Sekeletu and Mpepe did meet in conference, but Livingstone, who sat between them, unconsciously placed himself between the intended victim and the assassin at the appointed moment. The plot was betrayed by some of Mpepe's followers, and during the night Mpepe was "arrested," taken outside the village and speared to death.

Livingstone knew nothing about this until the next morning, and though he protested strongly about it, there was a bloody sequel.

Mpepe's father and another subchief had been involved in the plot, and in Livingstone's presence they were seized, interrogated, condemned, led out, cut to pieces, and their bodies thrown into the river to feed the crocodiles.

Seized with horror at being a helpless spectator to this trial and its terrible ending, Livingstone could only reflect that in civilized, Christian England, less than 100 years earlier, men had been hanged, drawn and quartered in as brutal a fashion in public.

By now, shocked with the scenes of savagery and heathenism he had witnessed, familiar with the physical discomforts of traveling in the unknown country, aware of the natural perils which might beset him, Livingstone was under no illusions as to what awaited him on his projected journey to Loanda. He realized that he had a fair excuse for abandoning the Makololo, but put the thought from his mind resolutely and planned to go forward, no matter what fate held in store for him.

Hazardous Road to Loanda

The immensity of the task that Livingstone was about to face was almost frightening. He intended to cross Africa, feeling his way from village to village, relying on his compass and the elementary lessons on navigation given to him by Captain Donaldson on his voyage to Africa thirteen years earlier.

With the exception of two colored Portuguese traders—who had previously covered nearly a thousand miles of the journey, but without making reports of value—no man, white or black, had ever made a way through the territory Livingstone was proposing to cross.

Part of his plan was to use the rivers and watercourses, to journey as far as possible by canoe, and then, when these had to be abandoned ultimately, to make the remainder of the journey *on foot.*

On November 11th, 1853, Livingstone marched out of Linyanti at the head of a company of twenty-seven bearers. All they carried on this perilous adventure into the unknown were a few ivory tusks—which Sekeletu owned—for trading purposes, a small supply of provisions, 40 shillings (about $10.00) worth of beads, some medicines, a magic lantern, Livingstone's kit of scientific instruments, a small chest of clothes and books (including the precious Journal), a meager supply of ammunition, three muskets for the bearers, a rifle and a double-barrelled shotgun for himself, a small tent and a horse rug. Had any expedition been more inadequately equipped than Livingstone's?

With the exception of the game that fell to his gun, Livingstone's staple diet during this exhausting journey, which took nearly seven months, was the same as the natives. Birdseed, meal, and manioc roots were the principal items. He soon found that his native followers were bad shots and wasted his precious ammunition, so that it fell on him to shoot what game was needed for food for the whole party. This was a doubly hard task owing to the difficulty he experienced in taking aim with his damaged arm.

The first obstacle was the Chobé River. This was crossed without incident, though some of his party were chased by a hippopotamus, from which they all escaped safely. Progress along the river was slow. Added to natural delays, protracted negotiations with strange tribes, and the recurrent severe attacks of fever, Livingstone was in an exhausted condition.

Incessant rain flooded the countryside and caused delays and detours. Everything metallic, including guns, rusted in the humid conditions; the canvas of his tent rotted; and his clothes became mildewed. Day after day he rode, walked, ate, and hunted in steaming dampness; night after night he tossed in restless, sometimes fever-torn, sleep on the sodden ground.

The first few villages and tribes Livingstone encountered had been friendly, but the atmosphere was steadily deteriorating. Chiefs became greedy and demanded tribute before they would let the white man pass through their dominions. Presently he entered the territory of the fiercest tribe in Portuguese Africa, the Chiboque country. At the first Chiboque village, he had a taste of what was to come when Njambi, the chief, surrounded Livingstone's party with a large force equipped with guns.

Livingstone, calm but quick-witted, was equal to the occasion. He showed no sign of fear, but set up a chair and suggested to Njambi that he do the same, and that they confer. He knew full well that no African could resist an invitation to palaver. With his gun across his knees, Livingstone began to reason with the native leader.

While Livingstone was talking with Njambi, his trained Makololo warriors gradually surrounded the Chief and his headmen. When realization dawned upon them that they had been outwitted and had themselves fallen into a trap, they allowed Livingstone to proceed unharmed.

Other troubles beset the explorer. On March 11th, while he was lying ill with fever, there were signs of mutiny. Livingstone seized a double-barrelled pistol and rushed upon the leaders, leaving them in little doubt that he was the master. The rebellion was quelled by his determined action, but his followers continued in bad heart, though they promised never to desert him—a promise faithfully kept.

By this time, Livingstone was so weak from fever that he had to ride on the back of an ox. At times he was so ill that he could neither ride nor walk, and had to be led by his men in order to prevent him from collapsing. It was in this condition, wet to the skin with the continual rain, his equipment sodden and rotted, that he reached the River Quango. Here, the chief of the Bashinje refused to let him cross, unless he pay an exorbitant tribute, demanding "a man, an ox, or a gun."

Just at the critical moment, when the demands of the chief were turning into threats, a young halfcaste Portuguese militia sergeant appeared and saved the situation. On his advice and under his guidance, Livingstone and his party moved down to the ferry. The Bashinje opened fire on them, but Livingstone and his party crossed unharmed.

When they reached the other side, they were on Portuguese territory, and safe. Here the young Portuguese sergeant, Cypriano di Abreu, entertained them hospitably, and furnished them with sufficient rations to journey on to the Portuguese trading station and fort at Cassange. On April 10th, clad in rags, his body skin and bones, completely destitute, Livingstone entered Cassange.

The officer in charge of this post, Captain Neves, entertained him in his own house, furnished food for his followers, and completely reclothed the traveler from head to toe. The same kindness and assistance were given to Livingstone all the rest of the journey to the coast.

A colored Portuguese corporal was assigned to act as his guide, and authority was given to requisition whatever supplies he might need. It was with great regret, therefore, that Livingstone had to oppose them over their policy with regard to slave trading. But Livingstone noted that so far as the Portuguese were concerned, there was no color bar; indeed, in this respect it is as well to read his own words on the subject:

"It was particularly gratifying to me," he wrote in *Missionary Travels in South Africa*, "who had been familiar with the stupid practice against color . . . to view the liberality with which people of color were treated by the Portuguese . . . The colored clerks of the merchants sit at the same table with their employers, without any embarrassment. The civil manners of superiors to inferiors is probably the result of the position they occupy—a few whites among thousands of blacks; but nowhere else in Africa is there so much goodwill between Europeans and natives as here. If some border colonists had the absolute certainty of our Government declining to bear them out in their arrogance, we should probably hear less of Caffre insolence. It is insolence which begets insolence."

As they neared their goal, Livingstone's faithful Makololo servants began to have misgivings. They began to fear that when they reached the coast they would be given into slavery. But Livingstone, though himself feeling a little unsure about the outcome, reassured them that nothing would happen to them that did not first happen to himself.

On May 31st, the little caravan stood on a hill overlooking Loanda. Livingstone was suffering from the effects of malaria and chronic dysentery—a poor, broken wreck of a man who was unable to sit on an ox for more than ten minutes. As he stumbled down the steep incline, he wondered what sort of a reception he would get from the British Consul there; he did not wonder for long.

As he approached the Consul's residence, he noticed the carefully cultivated flowers in front of it. This was all the reassurance he needed. He reasoned, rightly, that the man responsible for such a sight must be of a wholesome nature.

A warm British welcome awaited him. Mr. Gabriel, the Consul, noting that the explorer was a tired and sick man, promptly surrendered his bed to him, postponing all ceremony, and refused to hear any account of the expedition until Livingstone was rested.

After sleeping for six months on the ground, often in water, Livingstone accepted the offer thankfully. His magnificent journey ended, as he recorded, "in the luxuriant pleasure of a good English couch. I was soon asleep."

The Sounding Smoke

Livingstone remained at Loanda for almost four months. The hardships he had endured on his journey from Linyanti and the recurrent attacks of malaria and dysentery had reduced him to a mere skeleton, and it was some weeks before he was able to leave his bed. Mr. Gabriel nursed Livingstone, and a squadron of British warships called at the port so that he was able to receive attention from one of the ship's doctors.

When he was partly recovered, one of the ship's captains offered him a passage home to England, but Livingstone, loyal to the natives who had traveled with him through the unknown African territory and to a promise given to Sekeletu to bring them back to Linyanti, refused the offer. He spent his convalescent period in writing up his Journals and preparing reports for both the London Missionary Society and the Royal Geographical Society.

On September 20th, 1854, he started back on the return journey to Makolololand after a brief postponement due to a relapse of the fever.

On this occasion, he and his followers were better equipped. Instead of only five guns in all, each of the Makololo was armed with a musket. Twenty new carriers were commissioned. The Portuguese authorities issued the explorer with letters and visas to all commandments in the districts through which his route lay, directing them to render him all possible assistance. His followers, as well as himself, were provided with new clothing, and an abundance of supplies was carried.

Many of these items were supplied by public subscription, and Livingstone paid ready tribute to the generosity of the Portuguese, as well as to Mr. Gabriel and the members of Her Majesty's Royal Navy.

It was a happy expedition that set off on the long trail into the interior. The outward journey had taken seven months; the return journey was to take almost a year. The expedition was delayed, almost from the start, by attacks of fever on both natives and Livingstone himself, and in consequence, the caravan was able to march only short distances.

Without any hostility from natives, the expedition reached the Portuguese fort of Pungo Andongo towards the end of autumn. Pungo Andongo is about 200 miles from Loanda and is situated in the midst of a group of curious columnar rocks, each about 300 feet in height. In the early days of Portuguese settlement in Africa, in the belief that it was unhealthy, it had been a penal colony. Livingstone, however, found it to be one of the healthiest districts in Africa.

Here he became the guest of a slave-owning merchant prince, Colonel Pires. Apart from his ownership of slaves, who Livingstone thought were so well treated that they might well have been freely hired servants, the explorer held him in great esteem. Unfortunately, in spite of his intense desire to march eastward, his stay had to be prolonged because it was here that he learned of the loss of all his dispatches home when the ship carrying them, the *Forerunner*, was lost.

From October, when he received this information, until the end of the year, Livingstone stayed at Pungo Andongo and rewrote all the lost documents and re-drew the maps to illustrate them. On January 1st, 1855, his task completed, he left Pungo Andongo and set out on his journey into the interior.

It was at Cassange that he received news which affected him profoundly, for among dispatches received from home was included a copy of *The Times*, in which was an account of the Charge of the Light Brigade at Balaclava. From Cassange, he pushed on, meeting with friendship from natives and white settlers alike, though progress was slowed up by frequent attacks of sickness among his bearers.

On March 16th, he was attacked by a severe bout of rheumatic fever, brought on by being obliged to sleep on the rain-saturated earth. So heavy was the rainfall that the countryside became one huge lake, and the party formed their beds by building up piles of earth and mud on the ground, covering them with grass, and then trying to snatch what sleep they could in these trying circumstances, with no shelter from the steady downpour of rain.

For twenty-two days Livingstone lay ill in a native village, fighting with his Scottish will this agonizing illness, and while he was in this state, members of his party came into collision with the headman of the village. The tribe concerned was one of the Chiboque, who, thinking Livingstone and his companions were easy prey, began to demand all sorts of tribute. To bring matters to a head, Pitsane, Livingstone's native second-in-command, lost his temper and struck the chief. In an instant there was uproar, and even more exorbitant demands were made for compensation for the insult.

Livingstone refused to meet these demands. But the natives armed themselves and paraded in war array, uttering threats all the while, so he gave orders to break camp and move on. They had scarcely left the village when armed natives opened fire on them, and this was followed by an attack from both flanks. In the scuffle, some of the baggage was knocked from the porters.

Livingstone had been given a six-barrelled revolver by one

of the naval officers who had befriended him in Loanda, and seizing this, he staggered back along the column of porters, followed by Pitsane and some other of the Makololo. He saw the chief, ran up to him, poked the revolved into his midriff, and told him to go back to his village, and take his warriors with him!

The chief was frightened, and tried to say that he had only come in friendship. But Livingstone's lieutenant seized the chief's gun and saw that it had been fired. The natives closed in, howling and uttering blood-curdling threats, but one of Livingstone's followers drove them back with a battle-ax. After a brief exchange of words, Livingstone coolly turned his back on the chief and continued on his way, telling one of his followers to inform the chief that he was not afraid!

There was a brief moment of fear that the chief might be tempted to shoot the intrepid explorer in the back, or that his followers, seeing their chances of plunder leaving them, might be provoked into an all out, irresistible assault. But Livingstone's coolness won the day, and his party marched on unmolested.

There was only one other instance during the journey to Linyanti in which they experienced grave hindrance or hostility from tribes on their route. This was at the passage of the Kasai River, where the chief, Kawawa, refused to let Livingstone cross unless a very high tribute were paid. Livingstone calmly informed the native that he would cross in spite of Kawawa's orders and, furthermore, would neither submit to the exactions nor remain where he was.

Kawawa ordered his people to arm, and bloodshed seemed imminent, so Livingstone ordered his people to pick up their baggage and move on, telling his men not to open fire unless Kawawa struck the first blow.

Some of the party were apprehensive about an attack from the rear when they began to march. They wanted to fight, and refused to move. Livingstone, to induce them to retire, took the lead, mounted an ox and set out. So many of his party remained behind, however, that he jumped off the ox and rushed to them flourishing his revolver. Kawawa took to his heels, and his people followed him.

The porters picked up their baggage and started to march, but out of the corner of his eye, the explorer saw one of them raise his musket to shoot the fleeing chief. Livingstone, realizing that if this happened not one of them would be left alive, promptly clouted the man on the head with the revolver, and made him join the others.

The party marched into the forest, while Kawawa's people, watching them depart, discharged neither gun nor arrow in their direction. But Kawawa did not give in easily, and when Livingstone and his men reached the ford of the Kasai, ten miles further on, he found that the chief had managed to get an armed party there before him, and that the ferry canoes had been taken away and hidden.

Pitsane, who had sharp eyes, however, found where they had been concealed, and, as soon as it was dark, he "borrowed" one of the canoes so that the whole party crossed safely.

The following morning, Kawawa and his warriors appeared

at the river and were astounded to find Livingstone on the opposite bank! They watched in silence while Livingstone and his party made preparations to march on, but made no effort to cross over after them, and, apart from a few verbal insults, made no overt act. Pitsane and his companions shouted back thanks to Kawawa for the loan of his canoe, and the whole party marched on in high spirits.

Progress was exceedingly slow, and Livingstone recorded that his average rate of traveling was only five hours per day for five days in succession, after which time they had to rest. They never marched at more than two and a half to three miles an hour, while a day's traveling consisted, at most, of about fifteen miles in a straight line.

The villages he stayed at, or passed through, entertained him as hospitably as posssible. On many occasions he received royal welcomes, and the natives greeted him with singing, dancing, and gifts. Sometimes he would be greeted by a chief carried on the shoulders of another man, and this peculiar local custom always amused him. Provisions, fowls, and oxen for slaughter were given to him, and he felt ashamed that he could make no return.

But though the natives he was now meeting were kind and generous, there were other perils still to be encountered. Beasts of prey, alligators, reptiles, leeches, had to be guarded against. At one place, Livingstone was charged by a buffalo, the most dangerous of all big game; on another occasion the canoe in which he was being paddled down the Zambesi was overturned by a hippopotamus. With lightning speed, Livingstone and his followers dived to the bottom of the river and swam underwater to the shore. The hippopotamus attacks on the surface, and had Livingstone or any of his party tried to swim normally they would have been slashed to ribbons or drowned by the infuriated, though dimsighted, beast.

Another peril he survived was an attack by carnivorous red ants, which seemed determined to devour him alive. But throughout all these and other numerous dangers, the party continued cheerfully on its way. Every step brought the Makololo nearer home, and Livingstone was looking forward to meeting Sekeletu again.

Linyanti was reached in September, 1855, amidst great rejoicings. The whole tribe assembled to hear the exploits and reports of the party, and Livingstone records dryly that the incidents related by his followers lost nothing in the telling! One of the gifts sent to Sekeletu by the Governor and merchants in Loanda was a Colonel's uniform, which he wore to church the following Sunday. Livingstone remarked on this event that Sekeletu's appearance attracted more attention than the sermon!

When he set out on the journey to Loanda, Livingstone had left a wagon and several articles in care of these primitive people. During his absence Mr. Moffat had sent additional supplies by a party of Matabele—sworn enemies of the Makolo—which they had stored carefully on an island in the middle of the river, building a hut over them to protect them. Livingstone found every article intact and perfectly safe.

But it is to be recorded that though the Makolo behaved

perfectly correctly to Livingstone, they did not treat every traveler, missionary, or trader in such a fashion. Livingstone thought that much of his influence depended upon the good name given to him by the Bakwains, and as for absence of hindrance by tribes on his return journey to Linyanti, he put that down to the fact that they were more strongly armed.

Livingstone would now have been justified in making a march back to Kuruman for a well-earned rest, but his eager spirit would not let him consider such a course. He had noted the magnificent waterways the Zambesi and its tributaries provided, and he was anxious to see how navigable they were. He had met Arab traders from Zanzibar, and on their assertion that a practical route existed, partly by the Zambesi, to the east coast, he felt impelled to explore eastward.

On November 3rd he set out. He had plenty of volunteer servants and companions for this expedition. Sekeletu furnished him with plentiful supplies, as well as goods for barter and payment of tolls. Instead of a retinue of twenty-seven, he now took almost 200, and the chief himself accompanied Livingstone on part of the journey, as far as the town of Sesheke.

The majority of the expedition went ahead to prepare a camp, while Livingstone, Sekeletu and about forty followers waited until late in the evening before setting out. They had to cross a patch of land which was infested by the dreaded tsetse fly, and a night march was essential if the animals were to get through unscathed.

The start was not an auspicious one. An unusually violent tropical thunderstorm developed, followed by a deluge of ice-cold rain. With the baggage gone in advance, Livingstone was obliged to lie down, unprotected, to try to sleep on the wet earth, but Sekeletu, primitive native chief, rose quietly, covered Livingstone with his own cloak, and remained by his side all night without any cover for himself.

At Sesheke, Livingstone was given further supplies of oxen and trading goods, and on November 13th, the party set off down the Zambesi. Some of them, including Livingstone, traveled by canoe; others drove the cattle along the bank. And on this journey Livingstone heard about *Shongwe* or *Mosioatunya*, which he translated as "the smoke that sounds."

This greatly intrigued the explorer, and he prevailed upon the natives to take him to this place. He embarked in a native canoe, and, after sailing down river for about twenty minutes, came in sight of five great columns of vapor rising into the air about six miles ahead. The whole scene was beautiful. The banks and islands were covered with many different kinds of vegetation, and the trees were loaded with blossoms. He was the first white man ever to have beheld this view, and he was anxious to see even more.

About half a mile from the columns of vapor, the natives made him change into a smaller, lighter canoe, manned by paddlers well versed in the rapids, and in this he was brought to an island in the very center of the river. This island overhung the terrific chasm into which the waters of the Zambesi plunged. There was considerable danger of the canoe being caught by the currents and, missing the island entirely being swept over the falls, but the paddlers maneuvered their frail craft skillfully.

Livingstone crept to the edge of the island, and filled with awe, gazed down into the falls themselves, and the boiling, seething cauldron of the rapids below. Yet even in his elation at being the first European to have seen this wonder of nature, he made as detailed an inspection as he could, and estimated its proportions as carefully as possible with the primitive instruments in his possession.

His impression, confirmed by a subsequent visit to the spot in August, 1860, when he was able to take more exact measurements, was that they were the largest and most magnificent falls then known. For the first time in his travels he replaced the native name on his maps by a European one, naming it after his Queen—the Victoria Falls. Before he left, he laid out a little garden on the island, and carved his initials, together with the date, on a tree there. The garden soon vanished under the trampling of hippopotami, but the initials remained for many years, though they have now vanished.

At this point, the party left the Zambesi behind them and turned northeast, heading for the country of the Batoka. The scenery was magnificent, the climate healthy and invigorating, but the slave trade had cast a malignant spell over its peoples. Everywhere the tribesmen regarded the white man with suspicion, fearful that he had come for human slaves.

On one occasion, Livingstone was threatened by a frenzied warrior who walked round him for hours, howling and shaking a battle-ax at him. At another village, the chief, Mpende, showed fight, but the difficulty was avoided by Livingstone baring his breast and showing that he was indeed a white man and not an Arab or Portuguese half-caste slaver.

On another occasion, the caravan was charged by a cow elephant, accompanied by three calves, that burst through their center scattering baggage and bearers alike. Fortunately, no one was injured, though the elephant was wounded by a spear.

The party reached Tete, about 300 miles from the coast, early in March, where they received a generous welcome from the Portuguese commandant. As the season on the coast at that time was unhealthy, Livingstone was prevailed upon to stay at Tete for a further six weeks. Arrangements were made for the Makololo attendants to settle there, and land was assigned to them for the building of homes and the cultivation of crops.

Livingstone left Tete on April 23rd, promising to return and lead them back home, and accompanied by eight servants only, he went downstream by launch to Quilimane on the coast. Here he handed over his eight servants to the commandant until he should return and take them back to their people.

Sekwebu, his loyal and capable second-in-command of this march, begged Livingstone to take him to England, and after some hesitation and with considerable misgivings, Livingstone allowed himself to be persuaded. They sailed together on the *Frolic* on July 12th, but the weather was stormy, and in the rough seas poor Sekwebu, to whom the sea and the ship were strange wonders, went out of his mind. After trying to spear one of the crew, he threw himself overboard and was drowned.

The *Frolic* called at Mauritius, where Livingstone went ashore, to remain there convalescing from his various illnesses until November, when the P. & O. shipping company very generously accorded him a free passage on the *Candia* to Marseilles.

Yet even now, fate was unkind to David Livingstone. After the overland journey across France, he sailed for Southampton, where his wife was waiting to greet him. An accident to his cross-channel steamer caused him to land at Dover instead, and he had to travel up to London and then go by train to rejoin his wife, to whom he was so devotedly attached and whose companionship he had been denied for so many long, arduous years.

His father, who had been seriously ill, died only a few weeks before his arrival in England.

Both were events which weighed on him not a little, and he wanted to retire to some small place where he could be alone with his family for some time, however short.

To his amazement, he found himself a celebrity. The whole country was ringing with his name; he had become the focus of public interest. He was mobbed in the street by admiring crowds, and his features were a familiar sight in the national newspapers.

All this was rather irksome to Livingstone, who was by nature of a retiring disposition. When he had left England, he had no intention of ever returning, and he had directed all his attentions to African languages. He had spent three and a half years without speaking a word of English, and this, with thirteen years of only partial use of his native tongue, made him feel sadly at a loss.

Blazing the Trail

The statement that a prophet is not without honor save in his own country was certainly not true in Livingstone's case. His achievements were first recognized in Cape Town, and public demonstrations expressed the great gratitude of the people of that province for the work Livingstone had done—this in spite of the fact that, when he first landed there, a newcomer, young, inexperienced but enthusiastic, he had aroused considerable antagonism by his forthright theories on equalities of mankind irrespective of color!

In Great Britain, he was made a Fellow of the Royal Society, granted the Freedom of the Cities of London, Edinburgh, and Glasgow, and the town of Hamilton. In addition to the Freedom of the City of Glasgow, a sum of £2,000 (about $10,000) was raised by public subscription in that city as a testimonial to the services he had rendered industry and commerce by opening up new routes to the interior of Africa. The honorary degree of Doctor of Laws was conferred on him by Glasgow University, and other universities, including those of Cambridge and Oxford, granted similar honors.

The Prince Consort and other members of the Royal Family received him personally soon after his arrival in London, while religious bodies, learned societies, and chambers of commerce throughout the kingdom presented him with addresses. He paid a special visit to his native village of Blantyre, and his reception there can well be imagined.

But all this was extremely tiring, and Livingstone longed to find some quiet place where he could rest with his family, who were almost strangers to him, and write the book he felt impelled to publish. In a letter to a friend he states, towards the end of this period of public engagements and appearances:

"I finish my public spouting next week at Oxford. It is really very time killing, this lionizing, and I am sure you pity me in it."

Finally, he was able to achieve his desires, though he found the writing of his book, *Missionary Travels* to be a heavy task, in spite of the fact that he was well used to the pen. When he finished it, he declared that he would far rather cross Africa again than write another book.

For the first time in his life, Livingstone was supplied with ample funds from his own earnings, for the book had a tremendous success, 12,000 copies of the first edition being sold *before* publication, and the second a similar success. Half of the earnings went towards the financing of his next expedition, and the remainder he deposited in a bank for the benefit of his family.

At this time, Livingstone severed his connection with the London Missionary Society. There have been various reasons ascribed for this, and it has been suggested that he approached the Government to send him out officially as an explorer. The truth of the matter lies somewhere in Livingstone's reaction when he received a very tactless letter from the London Missionary Society which reached him at Quilimane. With the letter went the information that the Gold Medal which the Royal Geographical Society had presented him was retained at L.M.S. headquarters until he should arrive to claim it.

The letter went on to state that, while the directors of the Missionary Society appreciated the objects of his expeditions, nevertheless they were restricted in their power of aiding plans "connected only remotely with the spread of the Gospel." In the Society's opinion, it was not in a position to enter upon "untried, remote, and difficult fields of labor."

Livingstone, when he received this letter, was a sick man; he was exhausted by toil and nearly thirty attacks of fever; he was convinced, rightly, in his own mind that he had achieved something of value in the spread of the Gospel. Additionally, Livingstone had used up all his resources, stripped himself bare to cover the cost of his journeys, and the financial statement which accompanied the letter, showing a small balance due to Livingstone from the Society, was probably the final straw.

At any rate, Livingstone was exceedingly irritated by this letter, and in his reply, dispatched from Mauritius immediately before he started back to England, he said: "The proposition to leave the untried, remote, and difficult fields of labor as they have been ever since our Savior died for man involves my certain separation from the L.M.S."

Soon after his arrival in England, the Missionary Society voted him a special grant of £200 on account of the heavy expenditure he had incurred on their behalf, but in a letter dated April 7th, 1857, he declined this offer, and requested no further references to his supposed financial resources. In the autumn of the same year the Society was officially informed that Livingstone had decided against going out again under its auspices, and added that he was expecting Government support for his plans.

After nearly two years in England, Livingstone was appointed to lead a Government expedition into Africa to extend his previous journeys into the interior, to explore the Zambesi, and to pioneer commercial routes into that area.

In addition to his appointment as leader of the expedition, he was given the rank of Her Majesty's Consul for the East Coast of Africa to the South of Zanzibar and for the unexplored interior. Part of his Consular uniform consisted of a bluish-grey cloth cap with a gold band on a red ground, somewhat in the style of a yachtman's cap, and most pictures of David Livingstone show him wearing this headdress of which he was very proud.

Dr. John Kirk was appointed botanist and physician to the expedition; Richard Thornton, geologist; and Livingstone's brother, Charles, secretary and general assistant. Mrs. Livingstone accompanied her husband on this journey and took with her their youngest child, Oswell. The expedition was well equipped, and included a steam launch, which could be assembled from sections. The craft was named the *Ma-Robert*, the Makololo name for Mrs. Livingstone in allusion to the name of their eldest boy.

On February 13th, 1858, Queen Victoria received Livingstone in audience, and later the same day a great public banquet was given to send off the party.

The expedition sailed from Liverpool on March 10th, 1858, aboard H.M.S. *Pearl*, but when the vessel arrived at Cape Town, Mrs. Livingstone was so ill from the effects of the voyage that it was decided she should go with her parents to Kuruman for a rest before rejoining her husband at the delta of the Zambesi.

The *Pearl* arrived at the mouth of the Zambesi on May 15th, and put the expedition ashore after a short delay due to the difficulty in finding a suitable channel for navigation. But serious difficulties arose almost immediately between Livingstone and Commander Bedingfield, the navigating officer, and the latter resigned.

From the beginning, this expedition was one successive disappointment after another. A great gorge, the Kebrabasa, full of rapids and cataracts, presented an impassable obstacle. Livingstone and his companions were nearly drowned in a desperate attempt to shoot the raging waters, and he was forced to the realization that the route he had projected up the Zambesi to reach the Makololo territory was impossible.

On top of all these setbacks, the *Ma-Robert* (which the party nicknamed the *Asthmatic*), was a most unsuitable craft. A day and a half of hard work was required to cut sufficient wood to keep her boiler going for a day. There were frequent mechanical breakdowns, and worst of all, she was far from watertight.

Livingstone, finding the Kebrabasa rapids insurmountable, had decided to explore the Shire River in the hope of discovering the great lake which the natives said was its source. But the *Ma-Robert* defeated him, and his progress was arrested also by rapids, which he named the Murchison Cataracts after his friend Sir Robert Murchison, the great geographer.

A further attempt was made to ascend the Shire, and this time they reached the village of a chief named Chibisa. Here, Livingstone abandoned the steamer, leaving it in charge of two English sailors, while he and his companions struck overland in search of Lake Nyasa. The journey was trying. Sickness again struck the party, and the natives were hostile. But as a result of this expedition, which culminated in the discovery of a small lake, the Shirwa, Livingstone and his companions realized that the Shiré and Nyasa region provided the best means of access to the great fertile African interior.

Leaving this beautiful and luxurious countryside behind them, the party returned to Chibisa's village and sailed the *Ma-Robert to* Kongone for urgent repairs that she needed. The leaky craft arrived there on June 23rd, 1859, and there were further dissensions in the party, resulting in the dismissal of Baines and Thornton. Thornton subsequently rejoined the expedition, but died soon after.

In August, a third attempt was made to reach Lake Nyasa by the River Shiré. The *Ma-Robert* was again left at Chibisa's village, and the Livingstone brothers, together with Kirk and George Rae as engineer, accompanied by thirty-eight native followers, set out on foot for their goal.

Their route took them through the beautiful Shiré heights and through some of the most magnificent and healthy country they had ever seen. But there was ample evidence of slave trading; the natives were suspicious of the party, and open hostility was shown them. The constant guard against possible attack meant that the journey could only be taken slowly, and they found this very wearying. But on the morning of September 16th they were rewarded by the discovery of Lake Nyasa.

The party did not linger there, but hastened back to Chibisa's village. They arrived there in an exhausted condition, and at this point they divided into two groups. One, under Kirk, went overland to Tete, while Livingstone and the rest sailed the *Ma-Robert* back to Kongone for further repairs. The overland party, after many privations, including nearly dying of thirst, finally reached Tete. Livingstone's party reached Kongone at the end of the year, only to be greeted by bad news. The mails they had been expecting from England had been lost when the boat carrying them from H.M.S. *Lynx* capsized on a sand bar. Most of their stores likewise perished.

As the *Ma-Robert* was useless, Rae was sent back home to England to superintend the building of another vessel, and in the meantime, Livingstone made good his earlier promise to the Makololo to take them back to Linyanti.

It was a smaller party that he led back, however, and not all of them were anxious to return. Some of them had married and settled down at Tete; some had died through fever; and some had been murdered by raiders. But in March, 1860, Livingstone set off back to Makolololand, by canoe as far as the Kebrabasa Gorge and then overland by foot.

Wherever they marched, they came upon terrible evidence of slave-raiding activities—burned-out villages, skeletons of murdered tribesmen, terrified people. Added to this, the Portuguese half-caste slavers used the name of Livingstone, declaring that they had his authority to pursue their vile calling.

On June 9th, the party reached the Victoria Falls. There Livingstone was able to check his earlier figures, and he found that the falls were even larger than he had thought them to be.

They moved on to Sekeletu's town, Sesheke, and there found the chief living in strict seclusion, supposed to be suffering from leprosy. Sekeletu had deteriorated into a cruel tyrant, his tribes were discontented, and he had had a number of his subjects put to death on the suspicion of having bewitched him. Here, Livingstone learned of the deaths of a missionary party which had been sent to Linyanti.

On September 17th, Livingstone and his companions set out for the return journey to the coast. Pitsane, his able native second-in-command of earlier journeys, went with him in charge of a guard furnished by Sekeletu.

In the higher reaches of the Kebrabasa Rapids, Kirk nearly lost his life. The party was being ferried down in a fleet of canoes, and though most of them safely negotiated the boiling rapids, Livingstone's canoe was pulled by the currents towards a large rock. The steersman of Kirk's craft, intent on warning Livingstone, forgot his own peril and the canoe in which Kirk was traveling was suddenly capsized by the swirling waters. In an instant, the occupants of the craft had been thrown into the water. Fortunately, they were all rescued, though Kirk lost all his precious notes, as well as his surgical and scientific instruments—all he posessed in fact.

After this incident, the party made the rest of the way to Tete by foot, reaching the town on November 23rd. About a month later, they saw the end of the *Ma-Robert* when it was stranded on a sandbank.

Their fortunes were indeed low, but the kindly assistance of a Portuguese merchant saw them conveyed to Kongone after a brief stay under his hospitable roof. Stores were all gone, clothing was in rags, they had no news from home, their physical condition was poor, and in this sorry state the new steamer, the *Pioneer,* the construction of which Rae had been sent home to superintend, arrived on January 31st, 1861. With the boat came two cruisers, carrying members of the Oxford and Cambridge University Mission, eager to commence work in the Nyasa region.

Livingstone had decided to try to reach Lake Nyasa via the Rovuma River, and with the *Pioneer* specially built for river navigation, he felt hopeful that he would succeed. The Portuguese authorities were now alarmed at his activities, and were trying to close the Zambesi to all traders other than their own. Livingstone had to find a navigable waterway at all costs. But hopes based on exploration of the Rovuma were soon dispelled. The water was too shallow for the draft of the vessel, and after penetrating for about thirty miles only, there was an attack of fever among his officers, and the party had no option but to turn back.

Livingstone had promised to try to help the Universities' Mission find a suitable station, and though it hindered the work of the official expedition, he consented to accompany Bishop Mackenzie, who was in charge, on an exploratory trip among the Shiré heights.

From that moment on, Livingstone found himself in conflict with the Portuguese. The Manganja country, which lay on both banks of the Shiré below Chibisa's village, was war torn. The Ajawa tribesmen were harrying the villages, carrying off great numbers of the natives to be sold as slaves. The dead in the raided districts outnumbered the living.

Finally, Livingstone decided that he would intervene against the next party of slavers he met, liberate the slaves, and drive off the traders.

The village of a chieftain called Mbame saw his first excursion against the slavers. A long line of manacled men, women, and children came wending their way through the valley where the village stood. Colored guards carrying muskets flanked the line of captives, but as soon as they caught sight of Livingstone and his followers resolutely barring their way, they turned and fled, leaving their captives behind. Each of the men was linked together by a stout stick with a fork at the ends into which their necks were placed. Livingstone was told that two women captives had been shot the day before for attempting to run away, and that a man had been killed with an ax because he had fallen down exhausted and was unable to rise.

Fifty more slaves were freed by Livingstone two days later, and after establishing the Bishop at Magomero, he returned to the *Pioneer*.

While proceeding to Magomero, Livingstone and his party were attacked by a party of Ajawa raiders, and for the first time in his African travels, he had to open fire on natives. The raiders were driven off, only to return after Livingstone had departed for Chibisa's village. A pitched battle ensued, in which Bishop Mackenzie decisively routed them.

In January, 1862, Livingstone was joined at Kongone by his wife, who with other members of the Universities' Mission, had been brought up by the H.M.S. *Gorgon*. With the party came the little vessel that Livingstone had himself designed specifically for exploring the fast, shallow waters of the Nyasa regions. The little boat was called the *Lady Nyasa,* and the party had scarcely been transferred to it from the *Gorgon,* ready to proceed up the Shiré to join the mission at Magomero, when the terrible news was brought to them that the Bishop and his assistant had succumbed to malaria.

Fate next dealt Livingstone the hardest blow he had ever received. In November, 1858, while he was away on his Nyasaland expeditions, Mrs. Livingstone had borne a daughter, and it had been almost a year before he received the good news. Now, for a few brief weeks, David and Mary Livingstone were together again, but illness struck her. She died at Shupanga on April 27th, 1862, and was buried there in the shadow of the mighty Morambala.

From that moment onward, Livingstone became graver, more aloof, more single-minded in purpose. He felt that all he had to live for now was to put an end to the slave trade.

The *Lady Nyasa* had cost Livingstone, personally, the sum of £6,000, and before she was able to prove of much service to him the expedition was recalled. What to do with the little boat was something of a problem. The Government had made no offer to purchase her from him, and he was loath to sell her on the African Coast in case she would ultimately fall into the hands of a slave trader.

He decided on the sort of scheme that only David Livingstone could project and carry out. He decided to sail the *Lady Nyasa* from Africa to India!

For any landlubber this would have been an extraordinary feat. The *Lady Nyasa* was a veritable cockleshell of a boat. She was only forty feet long, with a tiny steam engine amidships, and an awning over the stern. With three white men besides himself (a stoker, a carpenter, and a sailor), and nine natives, seven of whom had never even seen the sea before, he set out from Zanzibar. It had been expected that the voyage to Bombay would take about three weeks, but he was so short of fuel that he decided to trust to sail, and on the forty-fifth day, after a voyage of 2,500 miles, the gallant explorer in his little craft crept unnoticed into Bombay harbor. Captain Donaldson's lessons had been well learned.

When Livingstone's arrival at Bombay was discovered by the port officials who examined the *Lady Nyasa's* papers and the identity of her daring captain disclosed, the welcome that was extended to him was very enthusiastic. But Livingstone was anxious to get back to England, eager to publicize the terrible subject of African slavery, so he laid up the boat, made arrangements for the maintenance of his men, and set sail for England by the first available vessel.

He arrived in London on July 23rd, 1864, after what had been, to him, a cruelly disappointing expedition, which had been overshadowed by great personal tragedy in the death of his wife. He was not to know that this journey was later to be regarded as the crown of his labors, and the piece of work he had completed to be of the most lasting benefit in the great continent of Africa to both native and European alike.

He had blazed the trail that others were to follow.

With the Slavers

On his arrival in England, Livingstone again found himself the hero of the day, and although the Government were inclined to be a little less enthusiastic about his discoveries, Gladstone, then Prime Minister, received him cordially enough. As soon as he was able, he went north from London to Scotland and rejoined his family. He had been away from home so long that his mother did not recognize him.

During his short stay in England, he did find time, however, to write another book. This work, an account of the Zambesi expedition, was completed in April, 1865, and was as successful as his earlier one.

But he had been chafing to get back to Africa. He had enlightened the British about the slave trade, and he felt a compelling urge to return to the country whose magic had ensnared him forever.

At the beginning of 1865, Sir Roderick Murchison, on behalf of the Royal Geographical Society, put a proposition to him: would he be willing to lead an expedition into Africa to discover the central watershed? Would he care to try to find the source of the Congo? Did the Nile enter Lakes Victoria and Albert in the south in addition to leaving them in the north? Where was the true source of the Nile? Would Livingstone be prepared to try to find the solution to these questions?

Livingstone was delighted at the thought of returning to the country he loved so much, and he was intrigued with the idea of solving these thrilling problems. Within a few weeks, the project had taken shape, and in a preface to his book, Livingstone announced that he was about to make a further attempt to open Africa to the influence of civilization.

His idea was to go inland, north of the territory that the Portuguese claimed, and in addition to assisting the Royal Navy in suppressing the slave trade on the east coast, to find routes for lawful trade and commerce and Christian missions. But the principal object of the expedition was the question of the central African watershed.

The Foreign Office were prepared to back this venture—to a limited extent. They made Livingstone Consul between Portuguese East Africa and Ethiopia, but their financial contribution was only £500 (about $2500), and he was to have neither salary nor pension. The truth of the matter was that the Government were desirous of keeping on friendly relations with Portugal, England's oldest ally, and were not prepared to spend money in saving African aborigines from slavery or slaughter. Furthermore, it was not anticipated—even by Livingstone himself, with all his unrivaled experience of African travel—that the journey would extend beyond a couple of years.

Livingstone's new commission was carefully planned by the Government to prevent his giving trouble to the Portuguese and their slave-hunting satellites.

The Royal Geographical Society also granted him only £500, in return for which they instructed him in great detail on what he was to do. Livingstone was annoyed with this parsimonious attitude, and pointed out that it was impossible to do what the Society wanted with such meager finances. Fortunately, however, his friend James Young gave him as much as the Government and Geographical Society put together. Without Young's assistance, the expedition could never have been organized.

Livingstone left England in mid-August, 1865, shortly after the death of his mother, and sailed for Bombay.

On arrival there, he was greeted by the Governor, Sir Bartle Frere, who was most anxious to help Livingstone in his war against the slavers, and the British residents in Bombay subscribed nearly £1,000 (about $5000) for the expedition, which pointed up the niggardly attitude of the official English promoters of the scheme.

Before leaving Bombay for Africa, however, Livingstone had two main tasks to do. First of all he had to get rid of the *Lady Nyasa;* and secondly, recruit the personnel for his expedition.

The first involved a great financial sacrifice. For the vessel which cost him over £6,000 (about $30,000) he was able to get only £2,300 (about $11,500). This money he invested, on the advice of experts, in the shares of an Indian bank, hoping that his children would receive the benefit. The proverbial bad luck which is forever associated with Livingstone's name still pursued him, for the bank failed and he lost every penny.

He recruited some of his personnel from African emancipated slaves who had been trained at the Nassick Mission near Bombay. He also took a detachment of thirteen Sepoys. These were chosen because they were supposed to be well disciplined and accustomed to marching.

Finally, all equipment ready, his detachment complete, he sailed from Bombay for Zanzibar on March 9th, 1866. Sir Bartle Frere arranged free passage for the party in a Government steamer, the *Thule,* which was being given to the Sultan of Zanzibar. With the gift went a letter commending Livingstone to the Sultan, and requesting that he be given every assistance.

It was a paradoxical position when Livingstone arrived at Zanzibar and paid his official call on the Sultan at the Palace. His Highness was certainly *not* pleased at Livingstone's return to East Africa. Many of his subjects were engaged in the slave trade, and part of his revenue was derived from the customs duties it paid. But the Sultan valued British friendship, and he did all that could be desired in fulfilling Frere's request. He granted a signed passport to the explorer, authorizing any assistance he might need.

Livingstone was in great spirits. His health had improved. He was, by nature, given to a sly sort of humor, though popular writings about him have generally shown him to be an ill-tempered person. At the official reception accorded him by the Sultan, a brass band blared away in his honor. As he departed, the band struck up "The British Grenadiers" and Livingstone noted "the wretched band struck up 'The British Grenadiers' as if the fact of my being only five feet eight inches tall ought not to have suggested 'Wee Willie Winkie' as more appropriate."

Seven weeks passed before H.M.S. *Penguin* called at Zanzibar to take Livingstone to Rovuma, the starting point of the journey, and during this period he filled up his complement of servants and porters. Among them were three whose names live forever—two for their great fidelity in his hours of greatest need, and one for treachery and cowardice.

Susi and Chuma were the two whose names are to be remembered with honor. Chuma was one of the slaves whom Livingstone and Bishop Mackenzie had liberated in 1861. The third, Musa, a Moslem native, had served in the *Lady Nyasa* on her voyage up the Shiré. He was of the Johanna people, described by all African travelers as thieves, rogues, and cowards.

Great astonishment was expressed that Livingstone should have included some of these riff-raff Africans in his party, and this astonishment, coupled with fears for his safety, was to be justified by events.

When the *Penguin* landed at Mikindany, twenty-five miles to the north of the mouth of the Rovuma, the expedition set out on the march full of exhilaration and high hopes. But this joyous anticipation did not last long. From the very first day of the overland march to Lake Nyasa, trouble commenced. The Sepoys and Johanna men outdid each other in untrustworthiness. They caused trouble by trying to avoid duty, and they stretched Livingstone's kindness and forbearance to the limit.

Within a few weeks, all the animals were dead of ill treatment and underfeeding, if not purposefully killed by the scoundrels who had been placed in charge of them.

Before a month had passed, the Sepoys had to be paid off and sent back. They were not only useless, they were mutinous; and they were capable of murdering their leader.

A few weeks later, when entering the territory of the Mazitu, a fierce Zulu tribe, the Johanna boys deserted under the leadership of Musa. Livingston was now left with but a remnant of his party—Chuma, Susi, a few Nassick boys and some porters he hired from village to village. But with the departure of the deserters, and rid of the Sepoys, Livingstone's spirits returned, and he increased his tempo of marching. Everywhere he went, however, he came across grim evidence of the slave trade, and as his line of march led him through a sadly depleted territory —through burned-out villages and ruined and desolated homesteads—the weather broke, and torrential rains, swamps, and persistent floods reduced his pace.

In the wake of the slavers, he found that the tribes were, if not openly hostile, suspicious of him. The villages were short of food, and his own supplies were running short.

To crown all, on January 20th, 1867, two of his little party of servants deserted, taking with them provisions, and—greatest blow of all—his medicine chest. The gravity of this misfortune can hardly be exaggerated. "I felt," he wrote, "as if I had now received the sentence of death."

This was indeed the case, though it was drawn out before its execution. He was certain to suffer from malaria, sure to experience the scourge of dysentery. Unchecked by drugs, the intensity of the diseases was bound to increase, and then, with his constitution completely undermined, there would come a time when neither medicines nor drugs would be of any use to him. His decision to continue into the unknown without medicines was tantamount to suicide.

On December 6th, 1866, Musa and his fellow traitors arrived at Zanzibar. They went straight to the British Consulate, and, claiming their wages, reported that Livingstone had been killed. At Zanzibar the story was received with great sadness, and the news was passed home. Livingstone, said Musa, had been attacked by Mazitu warriors. He shot two of them, and, in the act of reloading his rifle, was struck down by an ax on the back of his neck. The Johanna boys, who had been dispersed in the attack, had returned to the scene, buried their master's body, and set off back to the coast.

But Livingstone's friends refused to believe the story. Somewhere in the interior, plodding his way through fever-stricken routes, was Livingstone. They were determined to find him.

A small-scale expedition was organized by the Royal Geographical Society; the Government contributed ample financial assistance on this occasion, and under the leadership of E. D. Young, accompanied by Lieutenant H. Faulkner and John Reid, who had served on the Zambesi Expedition, set out either to prove or disprove Musa's story.

The truth was quickly found. The expedition established that Livingstone was still alive and continuing his progress, though at too far a distance for them to reach him. On January 24th, 1868, confirmation was received at Zanzibar by a letter from Livingstone. Other dispatches which he had sent by Arab traders had been destroyed *en route* and never reached their destinations.

As for Musa and his fellow traitors, they spent eight months in irons in a Johanna jail after the Sultan of Johanna had seriously considered putting them to death.

The southern end of Tanganyika had been reached on April 4th, 1867, and by this time Livingstone was so weak because of continuous attacks of fever and dysentery that he had to rest for several weeks. Throughout all this time he was ignorant of the furor caused by Musa's stories, nor did he know of Young's expedition in search of him. In fact, it was not until 1870 that he heard of it.

At first, he had intended to follow the great lake round the northeast, but the Mazitu were so fierce that he took advice from the headmen of villages and decided to explore the westward side instead.

Scarcely a day passed that he didn't encounter slaving parties; he was never out of sight of the pyres of smoke rising from charred habitations, or the bodies of slaves, who, too weak to march, had been abandoned by their masters and left to die in that great wilderness.

One incident left a deep impression on his mind. He encountered a mother and her little boy of three who were captives in a slave gang guarded by Arabs. The poor little fellow realized that he was about to be parted from his mother, and clung to her, crying bitterly. The price asked for him was *four yards of cotton cloth*. The child's feet were raw and blistered from being made to tramp long distances in the blazing sun.

But, surprisingly enough, these same Arabs, indifferent to the human suffering around them, inured to the sight of wretched captives linked or chained together, were friendly and courteous to Livingstone. Though they knew that he was fighting their trade with all his might, though he reasoned with them and strove to convert them, they furnished him with protection to travel through the hostile country. They equipped him with supplies and provisions, and generally saw to it that he lacked nothing.

Probably the fact that he was white caused them to assume a kinship with him. Nevertheless, it is a strange fact that without the aid from the slavers, Livingstone, their implacable and uncompromising antagonist, would have perished long before this from the privations that he had endured.

Mohamad bin Saleh, an Arab trader bound for the town of Ujiji on the east side of Lake Tanganyika, suggested that

Livingstone might like to travel with him. Livingstone was, by then, weary of his wanderings, and on December 22nd, 1867, they set off together, slaver and missionary, from Casembe, a town on the southeast of Lake Moero, bound for Ujiji. By March 17th, 1868, after a difficult journey in which they had to cover extensive areas of swamp and bogs, splashing waist deep through streams and swamps of foul-smelling black mud on the fringes of Lake Mweru, they arrived at a small native town near the issue of that lake into the Lualaba. This river, though Livingstone did not know it, was the upper reaches of the Congo.

Here, about one-third of the way to Ujiji, he received reports that Lake Bangweolo, an essential part of the river system he was exploring and mapping, was only about eighty miles to the south. Naturally, he wanted to go there, but Mohamad bin Saleh refused to accompany him. Most of his own companions, their thoughts set on Ujiji, deserted him, and weary though he was, Livingstone decided to do the journey alone.

With but four native companions, including the faithful Chuma and Susi, he struck back on his tracks. They crossed the hilly country, waded through marshes, floundered through tracts of spongy ooze infested with leeches. On their route, they were attacked on one occasion by a horde of drunken native warriors, who surrounded them and threatened them with poised spears, battle-axes, stones and bows and arrows. One false move would have resulted in the immediate massacre of the little party, who prepared to sell their lives dearly.

But Livingstone, in the old manner, remained still in the center of the blood-crazed natives, and displaying not the slightest sign of nervousness, gradually overcame the hostility of the natives and was permitted to continue in peace.

On July 18th, he and his faithful few arrived at Lake Bangweolo. The Livingstone tradition had been maintained!

"Dr. Livingstone, I Presume?"

In the early autumn, having completed a brief survey of the shore of Lake Bangweolo, Livingstone returned to Mpweto's village at the issue of the Lualaba. Here he found his deserters awaiting him, penitent. Livingstone took them on again!

While Livingstone had been thrusting forward to Lake Bangweolo and back, Mohamad bin Saleh had stayed at Mpweto's. He talked of going to Manyuema, westward of the northern part of Lake Tanganyika, abandoning the Ujiji march, and Livingstone, excited at the prospect of perhaps proving that the Lualaba was in fact the Nile, made plans to go with him. But the plan was abandoned, and Livingstone again reverted to the thought of Ujiji.

His means were exhausted; in fact, his exploration of Lake Bangweolo had been curtailed on account of his inability even to hire a canoe, so he had to sit and wait until he met an Arab trader bound for Ujiji.

Mohamad Bogharib, an Arab slaver who was particularly friendly towards Livingstone, offered him his caravan facilities, and at long last, on December 11th, the great explorer took the Ujiji road in company with Mohamad Bogharib.

The route they took lay northwest to the mouth of the Lofuko River on Lake Tanganyika, from which they hoped to proceed by boat to Ujiji itself. But before they were even half-way on the journey, Livingstone fell sick with the most serious illness that had yet attacked him. He had waded through rivers and streams, with water at times up to his neck. A few days later, he was down with penumonia, coughing day and night and spitting blood.

Had he been left alone with his faithful few, he would un-doubtedly have died, but Mohamad Bogharib saved his life. He watched over him, cooked his food, treated him with Arab medicines, and rigged up a litter so that he could be carried. For a whole month, he journeyed in this fashion, and when he finally reached the shore of Lake Tanganyika he was in an ex-hausted, greatly emaciated state, but still alive.

The last stage of the journey again depended on Arab assistance. The only canoes available belonged to the rich and influential Syde bin Habib. The canoes were forthcoming, and on March 14th, 1869, Livingstone reached his goal.

Livingstone's life was one pattern of disapppointment after another. He had been without medicines or drugs, and had lacked the essential quinine for months. When he reached Ujiji, he had expected to find the stores he had ordered, including medical supplies, awaiting him. There was no medicine; together with the majority of the stores, it had been stolen. This was the bitterest disappointment of his life. A small supply of goods had been left for him at Unyanyembe, at least thirteen days' march away. There were no letters or newspapers awaiting him. The whole countryside around, the territories between the East African Coast and the interior were full of war parties. The Mazitu were raiding other tribes; Arab traders were being attacked and killed by revolting villages; and, further south, the natives of Mozambique were in open revolt against the Portuguese government.

No wonder Livingstone began to feel cut off, alone, dispirited. Furthermore, he found that the Ujiji slavers were the vilest of the trade, and he described the town as a "den of the worst kind of slave traders."

After a fortnight at Ujiji, Livingstone's health improved rapidly, and he decided to set out again—in spite of the fact that he was ill-equipped and minus medical supplies—in an attempt to prove that the Lualaba River was the headwaters of either the Nile or the Congo. On July 12th, he marched off again.

He did not expect this expedition to last longer than four or five months. But once again he had underestimated the difficulties, not having taken into account the very real poor physical condition he was in. Two years were to pass before he returned to Ujiji.

The first fortnight of the Manyuema Expedition, as it was subsequently called, was easy going. He traveled southward by canoe along the lakeside for about fifty miles and then headed straight across for the western shore. By then, the journey had to be resumed on foot. He left Ujiji in the middle of July. By September 21st, he had established a camp at Bambarré, about 100 miles west of Tanganyika. And then came the inevitable setback. A sharp attack of fever, brought on by the cold and wet weather he had experienced in the highland country, laid him low, and he was unable to continue his search for the Lualaba until November 1st.

Three weeks later, he reached the Luama, a deep-flowing river, where he was brought to a standstill. The natives, suffering from the depredations of a slaver and ivory trader, Hassani Dugumbé, collected in force, and though they did not attack Livingstone, they made it impossible for him to continue. He had to turn back, and returned to Bambarré on December 19th. A week later, he had set off northward. He was determined, come what may, to finish his explorations and retire before the next year was out.

Six months later, he was back in Bambarré. The weather, the Manyuema mud, fever, rheumatism, and dysentery had utterly defeated him. More and more slaving parties appeared in the district, and finally, towards the end of June, his porters deserted him. Nothing daunted, accompanied only by his three stalwarts, Susi, Chuma, and Gardner, he set off to the north-west for Lualaba.

The tribesmen were in revolt with the Arab traders. No longer did they submit meekly to the superior armament of the slavers. They fought back. On one occasion, he passed through a string of nine villages, "burned for a single string of beads." The same day, camped near some trading Arabs, he reported that one was pinned to the earth by a spear during the night. The Arabs wanted to take their revenge, but the fortunate arrival of Livingstone's particular slaver friend, Mohamad Bogharib, prevented what would have been a general massacre.

The old Livingstonian optimism about finding a route to the Luabala through the northwest began to wane. He began to doubt its possibility. The country, though fairly densely popu-lated, was almost impassable. Flooded rivers, breast and neck deep, had to be crossed. The mud was appalling, and, to crown all, he developed ulcers on his feet. There was no alternative but to return to Bambarré, where he arrived on July 22nd and where he was to remain a further eight months.

Of the period spent at Bambarré, a third of it was spent on a sick bed, and he felt the need of drugs badly. In addition to the perils he had faced, a new and terrible one had spread inland from Zanzibar. A great epidemic of cholera had swept fast and far along the trade routes.

He had written to Dr. Kirk at Zanzibar requesting a new party of carriers, and on February 4th, 1871, they arrived. Ten of them were Banian slaves, and their first action was to go on strike until they received higher wages! They then stated that their instructions were not to go forward, but to bring Livingstone back to the coast. The situation was a desperate one, but Mohamed Bogharib intervened, and at pistol point, brought the malcontents to reason.

On February 16th, the little caravan set out in pursuit of the quest which had so long eluded Livingstone.

He started out confidently, and conditions improved as he went along. A cheerful note began to creep into his diaries at this time, and he was feeling better physically and mentally. Soon he had good news about the Lualaba. He was within six miles of this mighty stream, and he was getting near his journey's end.

But close upon this news came reports of heavy fighting in the north. A powerful chief, Luapanya, had forced a battle with Mohamad Bogharib. From the south came more bad news—Arab slavers had attacked a village and taken slaves. His fortunes were changing again, for his men fell sick, heavy rains set in, and mutiny was imminent. But finally, on March 29th, Livingstone gazed on the river of his dreams—a mighty river, deep, 3,000 yards broad, and rolling *to the north*.

Then followed several weary months. He waited at the town of Nyangwé, on the banks of the Lualaba, unable to hire canoes to cross the river, writing his Journals, waiting for something to turn up. The Manyuema people were hostile, and he could see no hope of getting away without Arab help. Fortunately, on June 16th, Dugumbé, with a large retinue and 500 guns, arrived on the scene, and proved ready to help Livingstone *at a price.* Livingstone's hopes were raised, only to be dashed cruelly when the Arab put him off persistently, and on July 15th there was an appalling massacre of Manyuema women, children, and old people by Dugumbé's followers.

Livingstone was an unwilling and helpless witness of this atrocity, and had to be restrained by Dugumbé himself from using his pistol on the miscreants. The slaughter was frightful, though Livingstone was able to rescue a few of the terrified natives. He was sickened at the thought that he had been helped by the very people who had slaughtered the natives, and this sickness of mind brought on sickness of body. But he resolved, small as his party was and in spite of the fever ravaging his body, to start off back to Ujiji on his own. On July 20th, he set off back through Manyuemaland. The retreat was terrible. He encountered hostility from the natives along every mile of the escape path. Three times in one day he escaped death by a hairsbreadth. His party were attacked in the thickest part of the forest, where an ambush had been laid for them. In the resultant hail of spears, one grazed his back and a second passed over his head by a scant foot. For some reason the attack was not pressed home, but they ran the gauntlet of jeers, threats, and curses thrown at them by unseen foes in the undergrowth, and along the route was the monotonous, spine-chilling throb of war drums.

At length, clear of the enemy country, they reached a little clearing, where Livingstone experienced his third narrow escape that day. A gigantic tree, which had been burned about the roots, suddenly crashed on him, and missed him by one yard. His own comments on this terrible journey are worth noting:

"I became weary with the constant strain of danger, and—as, I suppose, happens with soldiers on the field of battle—not courageous, but perfectly indifferent whether I were killed or not."

Livingstone's association with Mohamad Bogharib and Dugumbé had identified him, in the eyes of the Manyuema, with slaving activities. His life was in danger from the very people he sought to help. It was in a bitter mood, feeling that he had failed when almost within sight of his goal, that he arrived once again in Ujiji, on October 23rd, 1871.

Here, luck seemed finally to have left him. Goods and stores upon which he depended had been converted by the Arab sheriff in charge of them. The destitute Livingstone was visited by this rogue, who came to him with an oily smile and attempted to shake hands. Livingstone was, rightly, furious with the thief, and told him that had he been an Arab and not a Christian he would have cut his hands and ears off for thieving, a typical Arab punishment still inflicted today in the Yemen of Arabia.

He rested at Ujiji for a few days, wondering what to do. He decided to wait there and send to Zanzibar for help. But there was a sudden, thrilling, dramatic change in his fortunes. On the morning of November 10th, the faithful Susi came rushing to Livingstone.

"An Englishman, *bwana*, an Englishman!" he cried, scarcely able to contain himself. It seemed too good to be true. From the moment he had left H.M.S. *Penguin* in 1866, he had never seen another white man. Scarcely daring to believe Susi's tidings he sent him back to inquire the visitor's name.

Susi darted back down the street, and Livingstone went to the door of his house. The whole population of Ujiji were milling about in great excitement. The sound of guns being discharged and the cry of "Bindera Kisungu!" ("A white man's flag!") told Livingstone that he was not dreaming. He pushed his way through the crowd, and stood in the center of a semicircle of Arabs at the head of the main street. Flags and streamers were being waved on all sides, and presently, over the heads of the excited throng, Livingstone saw, indeed, a white man's flag; not the Union Jack, but equally as welcome a sight—the Stars and Stripes.

A moment more, and Henry Morton Stanley pushed his way through the excited crowd to where Livingstone stood, walked deliberately to him, took off his hat and said: "Dr. Livingstone, I presume?"

The Last Journey

Stanley was Welsh by birth, American by adoption, and a journalist by profession. Like Livingstone, he had great physical and moral courage, and, like Livingstone, the story of his life is a story of the triumph of will power over adversity.

Livingstone's disappearance into the interior of Africa, the rumors of his death spread by Musa, the fact that he was still alive—proved by Young's expedition—and the long silence thereafter, aroused the imagination of the world. The manager of the *New York Herald,* the son of its proprietor, Mr. Gordon Bennett, decided to "feature" Livingstone.

Stanley had established a reputation in the front ranks of journalists of the day when he had accompanied Sir Robert Napier on his expedition to Abyssinia against King Theodore. Mr. Bennett reasoned, rightly, that news of Livingstone would be a "scoop" of no small order, and decided that Stanley was the man to pull it off.

On October 16th, 1869, Mr. Bennett, who was in Paris, sent for Stanley and told him to find Livingstone at all costs. He was prepared to go to any expense to get the story.

Stanley was a little taken aback at the proposition. He knew nothing about the interior of Africa. He added that he believed, as most people did, that Livingstone was dead anyway. Mr. Bennett explained that the *Herald* would pay any price for news which would interest the world. He insisted that Stanley find Livingstone, but that it was not a desperately urgent matter and not to be Stanley's immediate objective. It was to be the climax to a very full journalistic program—what is, nowadays, called a "stunt."

Some idea of Stanley's program may be gleaned from the fact that his first task was to witness the opening of the Suez Canal on November 16th; on December 16th he was to interview Sir Samuel White Baker's expedition in Upper Egypt. Thence his tour took him to Jerusalem, Constantinople (now Istanbul), the Crimea, Baku, Teheran, and through Persia to Bombay. On arrival in Africa he made five caravan travels in

Africa, indulging in battles and fighting the King of Uyoweh. It was almost two years and two months to the day after he received his instructions in France that he found Livingstone at Ujiji.

The arrival of Stanley gave Livingstone a new lease on life. The medicines he brought and the company he made alleviated Livingstone's physical disorders. The news he told and the letters and newspapers he handed to him brought the zest of life back to him.

Livingstone had begun to lose faith in the outer world when Stanley had arrived, in the proverbial nick of time. In letters to Kirk, he had complained that he was anxious that his letters and correspondence should not be given to the public. He was concerned because four spurious publications had been concocted from his letters home. One had been sold in America as "the book" by a schoolmaster called Adams. In England, Routledge had sold a shilling book as his on all the railways in England and America, then offered Livingstone £20 (about $100.00) to keep quiet about it. A secretary of the London Missionary Society had joined in a similar piracy, and a second secretary of the same body had "performed a like villainy," knowing full well that Livingstone would not sue that organization.

Although he must have realized that Stanley was first and foremost a journalist, he was eternally grateful to him, and drafted letters for publication in the *Herald* describing and denouncing the slave trade.

It is little wonder that the two men got on well together. Livingstone recognized in Stanley a kindred spirit, and Stanley had a great respect for the older man. When, therefore, Stanley pressed Livingstone to return to Zanzibar, Livingstone felt that he wanted to be up and doing, and prevailed on Stanley to make an exploratory trip up Lake Tanganyika with him instead!

On November 16th, they set out up the Lake to see if the Lusize' flowed out of its northern end. In a long canoe, borrowed from the Ujijian Arabs, with twenty of Stanley's men to provide the crew, they paddled up the coast. On December 13th, they were again in Ujiji. They had solved the geographical problem. They had ascertained that the Lusize' flowed *into* the Lake, not out of it.

On one or two occasions, there had been very slight signs of restlessness by natives of the lakeside villages, but they had managed to keep out of trouble, and the journey was otherwise uneventful.

On December 27th, 1871, they started from Ujiji to Stanley's base at Unyanyembe, which they reached on February 18th, 1872. The Doctor was, by then, all in, and Stanley did all in his power to persuade him to return home with him. But his great ambition was to solve the problem of the source of the Nile, and he knew, in his sad state of health, that once he returned home he would be home for good. After four and a half months together, they parted at Unyanyembe—Stanley to return home, Livingstone to remain and complete the task entrusted to him by Sir Roderick Murchison and the Royal Geographical Society.

On August 25th, 1872, he left Unyanyembe on what was to be his last journey. His party consisted of sixty-two. There were fifty-seven carriers, mostly engaged by Stanley, and five trusty members of the earlier expeditions—Susi, Chuma, and three others. After eight weeks' journeying, it became apparent that Livingstone's health was unequal to the privations entailed in African travel. He felt tired and unable to make more than very small marches. But by December 20th, he was about eighty miles north of Lake Bangweolo.

His diary makes continual reading of illness and rain. The rivers ran deep, and the ground was waterlogged, so that progress became virtually impossible. To plunge and stagger across rivers and streams swollen by the incessant rain was now quite beyond Livingstone's strength, and he had to be carried pick-a-back on his men's shoulders.

And so it went on, day in and day out, until, on February 13th, 1873, they sighted Lake Bangweolo. The comparatively short journey of some eighty miles had taken them two months!

Livingstone was gradually growing weaker. He was never free from dysentery, and he began to doubt that he would finish his task. The northeast shore of Lake Bangweolo saw his party brought to a halt about fifteen miles above the issue of the River Chambezi. The whole countryside was a vast waste of water which covered it to a depth of more than four feet. In these desolate surroundings, Livingstone had to wait for several weeks.

It was difficult to get canoes, and without canoes it was impossible to make their way round the southern fringe of the lake.

On March 24th, after numerous delays occasioned by the duplicity of a native chief, Matipa, who promised to lend them canoes but did nothing, Livingstone was forced to raid the village. He left ten men to guard his camp, then quietly took possession of Matipa's village. At the zero hour, he fired a pistol through the roof of Matipa's house, and the chief promptly fled. Before noon he had returned, bringing Livingstone the desired canoes, for which he was duly rewarded with a gift of trade goods.

Two days later, after punting across the floods, Livingstone had negotiated the Chambezi and camped beyond it. But the end was now near. He was excessively weak, he could scarcely hold a pencil to make notes in his diary. The last eloquent entries in his journal read as follows:

"21st (April). Tried to ride but forced to lie down, and they carried me back to vil. exhausted."

"22nd. Carried in *kitanda* (litter) over sponge SW. 2¼ (miles)."

"23rd. Do. 1½."

"24th. Do. 1."

"25th. Do. 1."

The last entry he made, when he was so ill that he could write no more, was made on April 27th: "Knocked up quite, and remain," he recorded. "Recover; sent to buy milch goats. We are on the banks of R. Molilamo."

After he had fallen from his donkey on April 21st, his man made a wooden litter for him, slung on a pole and borne on the shoulders of two men. In this fashion, with frequent halts,

Livingstone was carried until he reached Chief Chitambo's village, and there his journey ended.

He was laid on his own bed under the eaves of one of the village huts to shield him from the drizzling rain, while his faithful five labored at building him a temporary house. By nightfall, the new home was ready and Livingstone carried inside it. Outside, at the entrance, a fire was lighted, and just inside the door sat a boy, Majwara, whose duty it was to summon Susi or Chuma if Livingstone awakened and wanted anything.

The next day—April 30th—Chitambo came to pay his respects, but Livingstone was so ill that he had to ask him to come back on the morrow when he would have strength to talk. Chuma and Susi tended him carefully, and during the night Livingstone called for water, which Susi brought him. About four in the morning, Majwara wakened Susi. In great alarm, he said that before falling asleep he had seen the "master" kneeling by his bed. He did not know how long he had slept, but when he had wakened the "master" had not moved.

Susi summoned Chuma, and they went together into the hut. In the dim light of a candle, they could see Livingstone still kneeling by the side of his bed, his head buried in his hands on the pillow. As he seemed to be praying, they hesitated to go in, desiring not to interrupt him. But they could see no motion, hear no breathing. Then one of them went forward, quietly, and touched his cheek. It was cold. He had been dead for some time.

The death of Livingstone was a grievous blow to the little band of faithful followers. They were stranded in the heart of Africa, months away from their own peoples. The news of his death was spread through the camp, and at dawn an audacious plan was resolved upon. Susi and Chuma were elected leaders, and it was decided to carry Livingstone's body and belongings *back to Zanzibar*. No primitive peoples are more superstitious concerning death and dead bodies than the Africans. To transport a corpse across Africa was a difficult, even dangerous task, but it was carried out with dignity, with courage, and with devotion.

His heart was buried in a tin box, and Jacob Wainwright, one of the Nassick boys, read the burial service. On a nearby *myonga* tree he carved the inscription:

"Livingstone, May 4, 1873."

Two strong posts, with a crosspiece, were erected to mark the spot where the body had lain. The tree has since perished, but shoots from its roots have grown up round the memorial erected on this spot. The part of the trunk bearing the inscription was cut out and brought to England in 1900.

Chuma went on to Zanzibar ahead of the party, and informed the authorities there what had happened. On February 15th, nine months after they had started from Chitambo's, the bearers of Livingstone's body reached Bagamoyo, where H.M.S. *Vulture* was waiting to receive the body. It was taken aboard and on to Zanzibar from where, with Jacob Wainwright, it was sent to England and reached Southampton on April 15th. On

132

April 18th, on a day of national mourning, Livingstone's body was laid to rest near the center of the nave of Westminster Abbey.

It was fitting that Jacob Wainwright should be a pallbearer on that last, solemn occasion. The others were Livingstone's companions, Sir Thomas Steele, W. Cotton Oswell, E. D. Young, W. F. Webb, his friend Rev. Horace Waller, Dr. John Kirk and Stanley. But for Jacob Wainwright, Susi, and Chuma, Livingstone's remains would have been buried in Africa, and it is regretted that when they had completed their last act of devotion they received neither thanks nor recognition from the authorities concerned for what they had done. But for the generous action of James Young who sought them out and had them brought to England, the world would never have heard of Livingstone's last days.

Thus passed one of the giants of an age, a man who had contributed much to the spiritual and commercial matters affecting Africa and the rest of the world. His intense loyalty and passionate faith contrasted markedly with the comparatively shabby and parsimonious treatment handed out to him by the authorities at whose call he had ventured on his last journey. In 1873, in response to public opinion, the Government voted him a pension of £300 (about $1500) per year. But, by then, it was too late, for he was already dead. By way of amends, the Treasury opened its purse and allotted a small pension to each of his surviving children.

The effect that Livingstone had exerted over Stanley was to turn him into a great African explorer, while other African travelers addressed themselves to clearing up the problems he had left unsolved at his death.

On May 1st, 1873, the day Livingstone died, the first move was taken to give effect to the campaign against slavery on the East Coast when British naval patrols were instructed to prevent the export of slaves from coastal ports.

Three years later, almost to the day, on the insistence of Kirk, the Sultan of Zanzibar issued a proclamation forbidding the conveyance of slaves by land under any conditions. With that proclamation, the evil trading in human flesh against which Livingstone had fought so earnestly and in which cause he truly gave his life, received a mortal blow. The Arab slave trade between the Great African Lakes and the Indian Ocean had been stopped at last.

Until the present day, the finding of Livingstone by Stanley has aroused much controversy. The fact that in the first place the expedition financed by the *New York Herald* was a stunt, coupled with the fact that Stanley made capital of his discovery, led to many calumnies concerning this great explorer. It has been charged that he deliberately made wandering journeys in order to throw other rescue parties off the scent so that he could find Livingstone himself! Furthermore, the fact that Stanley was an American and not an Englishman was received ungenerously in many quarters.

The plain fact of the matter is that Stanley *did* find Livingstone, was able to help him, did try to bring him home and help organize a relief force for him—things no other person had accomplished. To Stanley, we owe a great deal for our knowledge of Livingstone, and to Stanley it fell to carry on much of his work.

Of Livingstone himself, missionary, explorer, gentleman, there have been conflicting opinions. The Boers charged him with gunrunning and inciting natives to rebellion; the Portuguese assisted him, yet persisted in their slaving; the Arabs gave him provisions and protection, yet at the same time double-crossed him by destroying all his mail and stealing his stores.

But no man of any color, living or dead, has ever been able to utter a single word against his character.

In the gloomy forest regions, along the waters of the Congo and Zambesi, below the snows of Kilimanjaro, in the desolate wildernesses and on the open veldts, Livingstone is remembered as the friend of the colored man. Unreasonable he might have been in native eyes, sometimes cross, sometimes peevish; but he is remembered as being free from vice of any description, while his kindness and forbearance are ever green.

Perhaps Livingstone's own words give a better picture of the man than descriptions of even his closest friends:

"Nowhere have I ever appeared," he said, "as anything else but a servant of God, who has simply followed the leadings of His hand. My views of what is missionary duty are not so contracted as those whose ideal is a dumpy sort of man with a Bible under his arm. I have laboured in bricks and mortar, at the forge and carpenter's bench, as well as in preaching and medical practice. I feel that I am 'not on my own.' I am serving Christ when shooting a buffalo for my men, or taking an astronomical observation."

135

Credits

Designer/BERT RAY STUDIO

Illustrations by/PARVIZ SADIGHIAN

Cover Painting/MARY GEHR

Type/CALEDONIA

Paper/ 70# PUBLISHERS OFFSET

Printer/REGENSTEINER CORPORATION

Index of Place Names

N

W E

S

Congo

ATLANTIC OCEAN

● Loanda

SOUTH

Orang

Cape Town ●

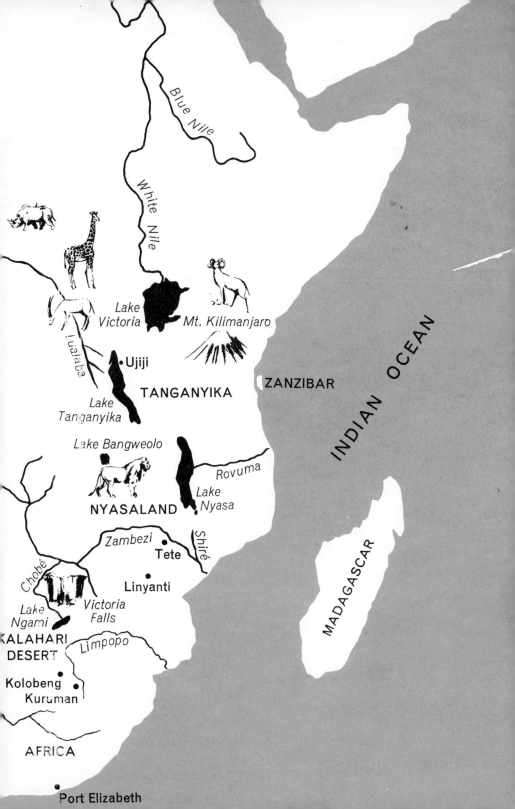

Blue Nile

White Nile

Lake
Victoria

Mt. Kilimanjaro

Lualaba

• Ujiji

TANGANYIKA

ZANZIBAR

INDIAN OCEAN

Lake
Tanganyika

Lake Bangweolo

Rovuma

Lake
Nyasa

NYASALAND

MADAGASCAR

Zambezi

Shiré

Tete

Chobé

Linyanti

Victoria
Falls

Lake
Ngami

KALAHARI
DESERT

Limpopo

Kolobeng
Kuruman

AFRICA

Port Elizabeth